THE LITTLE BOOK OF MUSIC FOR THE CLASSROOM

Using Music to Improve Memory, Motivation, Learning and Creativity

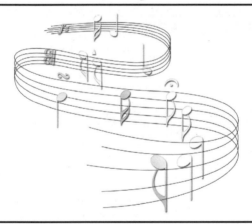

Nina Jackson Edited by Ian Gilbert

Crown House Publishing Limited
www.crownhouse.co.uk – www.crownhousepublishing.com

First published by

Crown House Publishing Ltd
Crown Buildings, Bancyfelin, Carmarthen, Wales, SA33 5ND, UK
www.crownhouse.co.uk

and

Crown House Publishing Company LLC
6 Trowbridge Drive, Suite 5, Bethel, CT 06801, USA
www.crownhousepublishing.com

British Library Cataloguing-in-Publication Data
A catalogue entry for this book is available
from the British Library.

ISBN 978-184590091-5

LCCN 2007938974

Printed and bound in the UK by
Cromwell Press Group, Trowbridge, Wiltshire

Contents

Acknowledgements

This *Little Book of Music* would not exist without the research and support of hundreds of teachers and learners who have implemented, tried and tested the theory and application of 'Music and the Mind'. To all of you, I say thank you.

Thanks also to my dear friend Sue Lyle of Swansea Metropolitan University who encouraged and supported my work from day one and continues to be my rock and motivator. To Ken Jones, whom I think of as 'The Man in the White Van', who sold me the Masters in Education course at Swansea Metropolitan University outside Marks & Spencer in Swansea because the modules were half price in the first year! Now Dean of the University, he is a true master of educational innovation.

To the GTCW which gave me my research scholarship to carry out 'Music and the Mind'.

To my Mamgu, who encouraged me to sing *Iesu Tirion* at the age of three and led me to discover that music was to be my vocation in life. And Tadcu, whose literacy genius and inspiration to mankind continues to this day at the age of 90. To my mother and father who bought me my first flute, and to Huw Phillips and Douglas Townsend for putting up with my continued thirst for musical tuition.

Thanks to those individuals who have offered ideas and encouragement that have kept the musical spark alive.

To Dick Hamer, who has opened my eyes to true happiness in the world of music, love and laughter, where jazz music continues to be a problem for me in more ways than one!

And finally, grateful thanks to Ian Gilbert, for believing in me as an educationalist, innovator and forward thinker, whose editorial skills have made this book readable, understandable and accessible. For my friends and colleagues at Independent Thinking Ltd, and to Crown House Publishing for their patience and understanding in putting together this book.

'Music is the medicine of the mind'

– *John A. Logan*

Let me start with a true story. I received an e-mail a few months ago from the wife of a primary teacher who had heard me speak about the many and varied uses of music in the classroom. Her husband had taken these ideas and thought them through professionally and properly. He wanted to have a go at using music in his classroom so he talked to his Headteacher about it, he talked to the children about it, he chose the music and the way he used it carefully and made specific allowances for those children who felt that it wouldn't help them learn. He then introduced a process of monitoring the effects and effectiveness of what he did. In short, he did things the way that Nina Jackson would be proud of.

What he found was that not only did the quality and quantity of learning improve but also behaviour was much better. Music used strategically and effectively was of considerable benefit to his classroom practice.

And then his Headteacher received the phone call.

One parent, one sole parent, one middle class, middle-England, *Daily Mail* reading narrow minded, bigoted, opinionated, did I mention *Daily Mail* reading, ignorant, close-minded, selfish, uninformed parent (alright, I'm biased here, and not just against the *Daily Mail*) was on the phone complaining about the use of music in their child's classroom and how it was getting in the way of their child's learning. The teacher was called to see the Head where he explained the findings of his 'musical experiment' and how the children loved having music in the classroom and learning and behaviour was improving across the board, including, ironically, for the child of the whinging parent.

Fortified by this the Headteacher explained to the parent what was going on and stood by his innovative teacher, allowing and encouraging the work to continue.

Then came the second phone call. Unhappy with the fact that their prejudices had been rejected in favour of the evidence, the parent had been on the phone to the Director of Children's Services in the local authority. Now it was that Headteacher's turn to be summoned.

And that was that.

Songbirds have been shown to have higher levels of dopamine when singing (especially when singing to a female), Java sparrows prefer music to sitting in silence, in Iowa bonobos have jammed with the likes of Peter Gabriel and Paul McCartney, and even carp can tell the difference between Bach and John Lee Hooker (which is probably more than our parent above).

Music seems to be part of the natural state of things, evolving in humans before language, according to some

experts (the controversial concept of 'ur song') and funda-
mental not to what makes us human but to what makes
us feel alive. Just like it is for the happy songbirds I mention above, as reported in a February 2008 *New Scientist*
article, whose singing induced 'reinforcement learning'
with a secondary function that 'may be to create a feeling
of euphoria'.

So, music can improve learning and create a feel-good
factor. But, of course, that would be *so* wrong in the classroom.

As Nina points out in this fascinating and practical *Little
Book*, music affects us body, mind and soul. The *New
Scientist* article says 'Musical activity involves nearly every
region of the brain that we know about, and nearly every
neural subsystem' and in his book *Musicophilia*, Oliver
Sacks quotes Nietzsche who said 'We listen to music with
our muscles' with Sacks going on to describe how music
can 'calm us, animate us, comfort us, thrill us or serve to
organize us at work and at play'.

Calm, animated, safe, excited and organised – who
wouldn't want a classroom full of children like that?

What Nina's research has shown – and she is undoubtedly
one of the UK's leading researchers and proponents of
music for learning and motivation – is that done properly,
music is a powerful classroom tool and this book is
designed to allow you quickly and easily to identify what
music to use, when and why.

And as if Nina's arguments and evidence aren't enough
(and if you want more detailed overview of her research

look at her chapter in *The Big Book of Independent Thinking* or go on to our website www.independentthinking.co.uk), here, based on my own experience, are eleven quick reasons why music can be of great benefit in your classroom:

1. It helps get the learners in the right mental state for learning

2. It helps get the teacher in the right mental state for teaching

3. It acts as an anchor - a direct link to feeling and emotions that you can tap into just by playing, for example, the theme from *Star Wars* or *Raiders of the Lost Ark* or (with your staff) *Grange Hill*

4. It has been shown to be effective in Accelerated Learning, especially Baroque music

5. It can bring a group of learners 'back down' if they come into your lessons over-animated, say from break or directly from a good drama lesson (or a cover lesson)

6. It can bring a group of learners 'back up' if they come in a bit too 'under-animated', say on Monday morning or directly from a bad drama lesson (or a cover lesson)

7. It helps with motivation, as a way of celebrating good work or behaviour

8. It expands horizons – world music proves there is more to recorded sound than Britney Spears

9. It can tap into their likes and values - youth culture and music being such close allies

10. It improves memory

11. Music we like, as it does for songbirds, causes us to release dopamine – the ultimate feel-good learning neurochemical

So, enjoy this book, play with music in your classroom, experiment, talk to your learners about it, talk to your colleagues, talk to – and be prepared to defend against – parents and let us know how you get on as you add a very special something to your lessons that really can help everyone feel more alive.

Ian Gilbert, Dubai
March 2009

Introduction
Music and the Mind

It was a dark and drizzly morning and the pupils, mainly boys, with various learning difficulties, were uncontrollable. They refused to settle for the start of the lesson. It was my NQT year and, as an inexperienced teacher, I tried every trick in my rather limited book to get them to be quiet: 'The Stare', 'The Wait', 'The Raising of the Voice', 'The Individual Coaxing of the Ring Leaders to Be Quiet'. But the panic was rising. How was I going to get their attention? I could feel my heart pounding in my chest. My career as a music teacher was disappearing before it had even started. This was the end, I thought – teaching was not for me because I couldn't get them quiet, let alone teach them.

Then inspiration struck.

My classroom contained a stage. I stood in the middle of it, feet slightly apart, digging my heels in to the boards as hard as I could. Hoping that no one would notice how I was shaking inside, I projected my voice as far as it would reach: 'Put your heads on the desks and close your eyes! We are going on a journey.'

Amazingly, the class fell silent. But there was no cause for celebration yet. 'Now what?', I thought to myself.

Reaching over to my collection of CDs on the shelf, I blindly took one down without even registering which it was, put it in the machine and pressed Track 4. I can still see the display all these years later, flashing at me, 'Track 4'. My future career hinged on this one track and I didn't even know what it was. I could hear myself praying silently, 'Not the Mr Blobby Songbook. Not the Mr Blobby Songbook.'

Obediently – or out of fear for a teacher who had quite clearly lost the plot – my unruly class lay their heads on their desks, closed their eyes and waited. My prayer was answered, for when the music started playing the room was filled with the most beautiful tones and musical colours I ever imagined. I had chosen 'Gabriel's Oboe' by Ennio Morricone.

And they were all listening.

When the track finished, I asked them all to raise their heads slowly so that we could share our musical journeys. It was at this point, when all pupils were silent, both willing and wanting to share their experiences, that I began to learn how to teach. The music had allowed me to learn about the pupils I was teaching and to share some intimate and emotional responses from each and everyone in that class. For the remainder of the lesson I learnt about the troubles and triumphs of each of those young people and discovered that teaching is about sharing and respect, tears and smiles, openness and privacy, the knowing and the unknown and, most of all, an understanding of each other. This was the power that music in the classroom could have, and I was hooked!

To this day I still ask myself: if it hadn't been for that entrancing music of Ennio Morricone, would I have walked out of that classroom and never returned? Did this one track change my life to one in which I not only survived teaching but came to make teaching my life? Was this track responsible for my understanding of the power of music in a desperate situation?

On that day I realised that a piece of music could drastically and immediately change the emotional make-up of a classroom and all the individuals in it. Thereafter, I wanted to test the theory and implement the idea that 'Music and the Mind' is a match made in heaven. This quest came to influence the rest of my life as a teacher. Looking back, it now seems obvious that music can enable teachers, parents and pupils to develop personal skills, to learn and share knowledge, and to cultivate a genuine love of learning. Then, I was groping blindly for the key.

That was 1992 and my first teaching post in a challenging school in Hampshire. Fast forward a decade and you'll find me back in my native Wales as Head of Music and Learning in Ogmore School, Bridgend, with a Teacher Research Scholarship from the General Teaching Council for Wales. Now I had the opportunity to undertake a specific research study into what I called 'Music and the Mind' and share with others music's amazing ability to change the way we think, instantly and irresistibly.

This book is a *Little Book*, which means that now is neither the time nor the place to share with you the full nature of my research. (Go to www.independentthinking.co.uk if you would like that, or take a look at my chapter in *The Big Book of Independent Thinking*.)

The results of this research have had a major impact on teaching and learning since 1992. Teachers and pupils are using the philosophy and application of Music and the Mind to raise standards of teaching and learning as well as for their individual needs, be it emotional, spiritual or for a specific occasion. The impact of Music and the Mind in educational establishments has been immense, and once you try out the suggestions in this *Little Book* you too will be amazed at their impact. I continue to seek new tracks, and many other individuals are more confident in choosing their own music as well as my suggested extracts to raise standards. Music and the Mind works because of the link between the neuro-science research and large-scale research work with (to date) over 5,000 pupils, the work in my own school, and teachers applying the methods in their own studies. This has been a long-term study since 1992 and I continue to collect and analyse data about the effects of music on individuals.

Such positive feedback was not only matched by the students' own account of the effects of music on their learning but also by the parents. Some had observed a more positive attitude to work, even towards homework. Some fed back that the behaviour of their children had also changed. When they became frustrated or anxious about home circumstances, the children asked their parents to put on some calm music for relaxation. Occasionally, if there was a family row, some children asked the parents to calm down and listen to the music! One family even told me how their child had helped save their marriage. The child had told them both to sit down, calm down and stop shouting at each other, instructed them to listen to a piece of music which was relaxing and calming, then asked them to talk about issues in a sensible manner, without raising their voices. Both parents were stunned, to say the least.

The common theme running through this book is '*Sound Waves Make Brain Waves*'. As well as rearranging your neural networks, music plays with your state of mind as the electrical energy generated by firing neurons creates Brain Waves. The alpha, beta, theta and delta frequencies created by neural activity – Brain Waves – determine what functions you're best able to carry out and conduct at that moment in time. The right music at the right time travelling through the air creates these sound waves which in turn alter or affect the Brain Waves. The music you listen to can influence the waves' frequency, and so your state of mind. And not only does the music affect your mind, it also changes the state of your body. Your autonomic nervous system is literally the link between your mental and physical self, and music directly affects its workings.

From calming unruly pupils to improving your grades to maintaining harmony in the home to saving your marriage – music really is, as multiple intelligence guru Professor Howard Gardner declares, 'the master intelligence'.

This *Little Book of Music for the Classroom* draws on my research and experience of using music in my classroom on a daily basis. It is designed to be a handy teacher's desk drawer-size guide to which music to use, and when and how to use it. It is divided into a number of chapters according to what you want to achieve at any given time. It also gives details of the music I use for these different outcomes, although I'm sure you will soon start to add your own ideas from your personal library.

I hope that it will help you get the best out of your learners and yourself, and that music will start to become a truly powerful learning tool throughout your school.

Chapter 1:
Music for Learning, Memory and Focus

Overview

In this chapter you will learn about the use of music as a tool to support your teaching and for raising standards of learning. This chapter is specifically dedicated to memory recall and priming the brain for learning in Ready, Steady, Listen and Learn, solving problems in Solve It Through Music, developing language, literacy, oracy and learning for special educational needs in Listening for Language and Learning, and music to support learners with study and revision skills in Smart Study.

Using music specifically dedicated to learning is an area which seems to cause the most controversy with teachers. However, seventeen years of research has shown that using techniques linked with the theory of 'Sound Waves Makes Brain Waves' has helped learners raise their standards of learning. You can find the data to support this research in *The Big Book of Independent Thinking*[1] in the chapter Music and the Mind.

The main focus of this chapter is getting the brain ready for learning – ready to recall information, to solve problems, to learn by rote, to develop study and revision skills and even deduce theorems. I've found that Focusing Music can help learners and teachers with abstract reasoning, brainwork such as analytical, creative or administrative thinking and aspects of motivation. Music has the neural firepower to jazz up your thought processes and reasoning skills. Listening to music can help learners encode information and improve the recall process. The right music at the right time can induce a mood of concentration, filter out any distractions, and structure thoughts for academic learning.

Music can help you work smarter, not harder. The accelerated learning school pioneered by Bulgarian psychologist Georgi Lozanov during the 1950s and 1960s, and then popularised in the USA by Sheila Ostrander and Lynn Shroeder, holds that learning in time to music at about 60 Beats Per Minute (BPM) helps imprint material in your memory with less conscious effort. Learning to music is certainly an improvement on the usual grinding process of silent memorisation; so why shouldn't something that sounds good make your memory work better?

Sound Waves Make Brain Waves – and with the right music, learners will have a tool that has been proven to raise standards of learning. This *Little Book of Music* is a tool for you to use and try things out. Hundreds of teachers already have – so give it a go!

The following chapters provide a step-by-step guide to help you implement these ideas.

Ready, Steady, Listen and Learn

Memory Recall

Certain kinds of music induce a receptive mood that generally enhances cognitive processing, can serve as a mnemonic memory aid to help you encode information in the mind, and supports initial learning, recall, and transference into working memory.

Music primes your mind for learning, whether you are deducing mathematical theorems, drawing conclusions from experiments, playing chess, or challenged by any abstract thinking. By using music correctly you will be able to stimulate aspects of the 'left brain' in order to promote logical and analytical thinking, as well as stimulating 'right brain' thinking to help you grasp the big picture and think in a non-verbal, more creative way. Music also helps when you are studying for a test or examination, for times when you need to recall knowledge, information, shapes or pictures. By following the guidelines in this book you will develop skills and processes to recall almost anything.

Try this for yourself: select a piece of music from the list at the end of the chapter and listen to it while you are engaged in a task, such as remembering the names of Tudor monarchs or the planets of the solar system in the correct order, etc.

1. Mercury
2. Venus
3. Earth
4. Mars
5. Jupiter
6. Saturn
7. Uranus
8. Neptune
9. Pluto

By linking a piece of music, or melody, from one of the tracks, the pupils make an instant link between the information they have been studying and the music they have heard. It acts as a 'brain trigger', much like storing information in a little box.

How to do this in the classroom

Listening Stage 1

- Explain that you are going to use music to assist with memory recall of a piece of work. Present the information you want the pupils to learn, for example using a handout, worksheets or on a computer.

- Having done that, explain to the pupils that when the music starts they should listen to it with their eyes closed and to follow the 'shape' of the melody. They can put their heads on the desks if that helps them feel safe when their eyes are closed.

- Now, play the music (for between 2–10 minutes). The pupils must *not* write anything down at this point – they just listen to the music and become engrossed in it. This will link the music to the learning.

Listening Stage 2

- When you finish demonstrating the musical extract, ask the pupils to choose a suitable way of remembering the information. They may use jotting, noting, drawing, bullets, learning diary or any other preferred form of note-taking.

- Now play the same extract continuously as they perform this task, again enhancing the link between the learning and the music.

- Towards the end of the lesson, play the music one more time (volume level on low) and get the pupils to show or tell you what it is they can recall, either as groups or individuals. Here, you will see how the music has linked with Memory Recall.

Hearing the music again will support the pupils linking and accessing the information stored in the memory linked with *Sound Waves Make Brain Waves*.

Listening Stage 3

- To see what pupils can recall in a follow-up lesson, play the same extract again and assess how much they remember. Don't leave it too long – as memories may fade. Linked learning is the key!

- If the pupils require continued revision and recall for their personal study of this learning exercise, give them the name of the musical extract and where they can get it themselves – for free (*see Appendix A*)!

- It is important that you note the date, time and task presented with this musical extract, as you do not want to play the same musical extract again to learn and recall different information.

Suggested Musical Extracts to Use for Memory Recall

These extracts are chosen because they are between 80-120 BPM and the timbres, textures and frequencies support Memory Recall because sound pulses at this rate create alpha waves associated with concentration and meditative states.

Mozart Musical Extracts:

Piano Concerto No. 21: Andante
Divertimento No. 15: Adagio
Adagio for Violin and Orchestra
String Quartet No. 21: Andante
Serenade No. 10: 'Gran Partita' Adagio
Eine Kleine Nachtmusik: Romance
Flute and Harp Concerto: Andantino
Piano Concerto No. 23: Adagio
Flute Quartet No. 1: Adagio
Violin Concerto No. 3: Adagio
Divertimento No. 2: Adagio
Clarinet Concerto: Adagio

Music for Learning and Focus: Memory Recall

Adolph Adam – 'Valse' from *Giselle*

Geoffrey Burgon – Soundtrack from *Brideshead Revisited*: 'Julia'

Geoffrey Burgon – Soundtrack from *Brideshead Revisited*: 'Sebastian Against the World'

Geoffrey Burgon – Soundtrack from *Brideshead Revisited*: 'The Hunt'

Fauré – 'Pavane': Modern version from Utopia

Jean Michel Jarre: 'Oxygene 2'

Mozart – 'Eine Kleine Nachtmusik': Allegro

Mozart – Symphony No. 35: 3rd Mvt

Mozart – Serenade in D Major: 3rd Mvt

Mozart – Serenade in D Major: 1st Mvt 1

Mozart – Divertimento in D Major

Robert Prizeman – Libera: 'Mysterium'

Franz Schubert – 'Rosamunde'

Liquid – Sweet Harmony – (original mix)

Vivaldi – Flute Concerto in D: Allegro

Vivaldi –Concerto in C Major for 2 Trumpets

REMEMBER

Sound Waves Make Brain Waves with Memory Recall when you:

- Choose the right extract using 80–120 BPM.

- Teach what needs to be learnt without the music.

- Play the music, pupils listen – get the pupils to follow the shape of the music.

- Allow the pupils to work while the extract plays again.

- Pupils review and revise what has been learnt and recall by playing the extract once again.

- During a later lesson, play the extract one more time to link the learning with the music.

- Then – Eureka!

Solve It Through Music

Problem Solving

You can use music extremely effectively as an aid to solving problems and for working on lengthy projects. For solving a problem you need to be in the right mental state. You need to be thinking creatively – musing and free-flowing. By associating a particular piece of music, you have an easy way to recall what was in your mind whenever you need to. Just play the music again.

By using the same piece of music on a regular basis – daily or even weekly, depending on the scope of the project – the learners will soon be able to readily access their own creative abilities whenever they choose. When they hear the music again, the learners recall their previous ideas – all the information and their own knowledge of what to do – so that they can then rearrange it and come up with new ways of thinking about it.

You could see this way of getting familiar with your own internal processing as a form of incubation. Each moment of realisation – the eureka moment of success – will then add to the positive effect of the music.

However, don't overdo it – don't expect miracles simply by playing the same piece of music over and over again. Best not to use any music for longer than ten minutes at a time, because then the focus may have shifted, the attention drifted, and you'll be associating it with other states – such as boredom or other distracting thoughts about what happened last night. And that will devalue the ability of that particular piece of music for developing effective brain tuning.

How to do this in the classroom

Listening Stage 1

- Choose your musical extract from the suggested list. (Do *not* use an extract with lyrics when problem solving.)

- Set the scene. Tell the pupils about the task they are going to perform and that soon they will receive more detailed information, but while they are thinking about the problem you are going to play them a piece of music which supports the problem solving process.

- Play a short extract so that they know what's coming and let them know that you will inform them when it's time to begin the task.

- Present the problem or task in hand. For example, 'What I want you to do is to find a way to build a bridge which supports a pencil case using only one piece of paper'. Set clear expectation of *what* you want the learners to solve and *how* you want the solution presented, and provide them with any handouts or additional materials they need to complete the task.

Listening Stage 2

- Make sure you have the musical extract ready to play when you want the pupils to begin the task.

- Inform the pupils of the length of time they have for the task, that they will be working silently for the length of the task, and let them know the length of the musical extract.

- Tell the pupils to get comfortable, and to make sure they have all they need for working on the problem – pens, paper and so on.

- Allow the music to play for about half a minute, and then indicate to the pupils that they can begin. Allow the music to play continuously throughout the task.

- One minute before the end of the task, tell the pupils that they have one minute remaining to complete it.

- Give the class a moment to reorient themselves and then ask for their results.

- Allow sufficient time to discuss the proposed solutions, collate the information and assess how the problem has been solved.

Listening Stage 3

- Make a note of which musical track you used. You can use this again in the future when you are working with Problem Solving tasks; the pupils will also make a link with it.

- Suggest that they might choose to use it themselves with problem solving tasks at home. Offer the name of the extract to pupils – and let them know where they can get it for free! Remind the pupils of *Sound Waves Make Brain Waves* so they can understand the connection and why you choose to use music.

Suggested Musical Extracts to Use with Problem Solving

These extracts are chosen because the textures, timbres and frequencies support problem solving activity. They have 80–120 BPM and this increases the learning noradrenaline.

Music for Problem Solving

Adolph Adam – 'Valse' from *Giselle*

Edmund Angerer – 'Toy Symphony'

David Arkenstone – 'In the Wake of the Wind'

J. S. Bach –Suites for Orchestra 1–4 – BWV 1066-69

Beethoven – 'Egmont Overture'

Beethoven – Piano Concerto No. 5: Opus 73

Geoffrey Burgon – Soundtrack from *Brideshead Revisited*: 'Julia'

Geoffrey Burgon – Soundtrack from *Brideshead Revisited*: 'Sebastian Against the World'

Geoffrey Burgon – Soundtrack from *Brideshead Revisited*: 'The Hunt'

Debussy – 'La Mer'

Debussy – 'Claire de Lune'

Fauré – 'Pavane': Modern version from Utopia

Jean Michel Jarre – 'Oxygene 2'

Robert Miles – 'Children': Original Version ('Dreamland')

Mozart – Violin Concerto No. 3: Adagio

Mozart – 'Eine Kleine Nachtmusik': Allegro

Mozart – Piano Concerto No. 27 in B-Flat Major K595

Mozart – Symphony No. 35: 3rd Mvt

Mozart –Adagio for Violin and Orchestra

Mozart – Serenade in D Major: 3rd Mvt

Mozart – Serenade in D Major: 1st Mvt 1

Mozart – Divertimento in D Major

Robert Prizeman – Libera: 'Mysterium'

Franz Schubert – 'Rosamunde'

J Strauss – 'Blue Danube Waltz'

R Strauss – 'Also Sprach Zarathustra': Theme from *2001: A Space Odyssey*

Liquid – 'Sweet Harmony' – 'Beloved' (original mix)

Tchaikovsky – 'Waltz' from *Swan Lake*

Vivaldi – Flute Concerto in D: Allegro

Vivaldi – Concerto in C Major for 2 Trumpets

John Williams – Soundtrack from *A.I.* 'Where Dreams Are Born'

John Williams – Soundtrack from *Schindler's List*: 'Theme from Schindler's List'

Hans Zimmer – Soundtrack from *Gladiator*: 'Now We Are Free'

REMEMBER

Sound Waves Make Brain Waves with Problem Solving when you:

- Choose the right extracts using 80–120 BPM.

- Present the problem and indicate in what format you would like the answers to be presented.

- Play the music for 30 seconds to set the scene.

- Then play the music again (all of it) whilst the pupils solve the problem.

- Lyrics are a no-no here if they are presenting the problem through words.

- Share the name of the extract with the pupils.

Listening for Language and Learning

Speech and Oracy

Think of language and communication as forms of music! Every speech pattern has its own rhythm, its cadences, its music – language has sound waves, too, remember. Every culture has its own songs, and learning to sing the songs of another culture will provide an insight into the way your pupils perceive the world and the music of their lives.

You can use music as an invaluable tool in the classroom for helping pupils develop their language skills – whether in learning new languages or in developing skills in their mother tongue. Play some music and get the class to listen carefully to the rhythm, noting how the beats are grouped together in time, and how the patterns and emphasis change from one group to the next.

Play some examples of various languages and listen for the different rhythms and music that is apparent in speech. It doesn't take long before you'll be able to recognise a speaker's language from the way it sounds. Getting these patterns right is a major step in learning to speak a foreign language such as French, German or Spanish, and even Latin, Mandarin and my mother tongue, Welsh. Picking up the way native speakers talk can initially be quite challenging, as it will be different from the way you normally speak – you literally have to learn to sing a different song!

For those learners needing to develop oracy, listening to or singing specific songs can be a superb way of addressing or even eradicating speech problems such as stammering, or a hesitation in connecting with other people. This kind of practise will also help those pupils who find it difficult to communicate through the spoken word. I have found it to be particularly effective for learners with dyslexia and dyspraxia.

Use these extracts in your lessons in any way that you feel will help your learners become more stimulated, more motivated and energised as they develop their thinking processes. If you are engaged in teaching a specific foreign language, choose songs from one of the lists at the end of the chapter.

As the teacher and provider of learning stimuli you will be in the best position to judge how much you need to change the environmental make-up of your classroom or learning space when working with these songs. You could be playing a song as the learners enter and then ask key questions about its content: which words they recognise, what the song is about. You can also use the song for learning vocabulary, and for developing the pupils' spoken or singing competence.

What do I need to do?

• Decide the primary purpose for using the particular music. Make a note of the link between the specific learning task and the music.

- Explain to the learners why you are using specific songs for teaching vocabulary or setting the scene for the language lesson.

- When you are using the songs to improve speech, focus on getting the class involved. If they are of an appropriate age you can explain its learning objective, which is to help them learn vocabulary or to create sentences through the use of rhyme or song.

- Make it clear to the learner what you expect them to do: how you want them to listen, what they should pay particular attention to, and what it is you want them to say or sing.

How to do this in the classroom

Listening Stage 1

- Use your chosen tracks at the beginning of the lesson either as the students enter or to set the scene for learning.

- Engage the learners in singing the songs when appropriate by getting them to listen to them once. Make sure you have the lyrics available: on a handout, projected on a wall, or if presenting them to SEN pupils, appropriate coloured paper (I've found blue is best!).

- Prime the learners by telling them what you want them to do: sing along, recognise key words and vocabulary, or spot the language.

- Play the music again during the set task.

Listening Stage 2

- When you have finished playing the music, play it again, in order to revise the learning. Sometimes you will need to play and/or sing the tracks several times.

  Rote learning combined with music is an excellent method of memory recall for language work.

What next?

- Make sure you note the date, time and task you gave to go with this extract, as you do not want to play the same piece again for a different task.

- If you intend to use certain tracks for particular types of language or oracy lessons, then pupils will come to associate the music with what they have to do. In this way, the learners develop a routine which is primed by the music – they know the type of activity you are giving or presenting to them, and know what to do. Hearing the music, they know what's coming next!

Here are different tracks for different purposes in developing Language and Oracy.

The rhythm of rhyme and music will be stored as if teaching by rote. Music with lyrics can stimulate your verbal imagination and trigger cognitive associations; words and music work together to activate both sides of the brain, resulting in special interhemispheric insight. This will create theta waves which are associated with creativity and imagination. Music at 80–120 BPM with these songs will enhance language and oracy.

The extracts below are chosen because of their impact on the language and vocabulary as well as being able to support learners with speech difficulties. See the end of the track lists for music that I have found helpful for dyslexia and dyspraxia.

Suggested Musical Extracts for Language Teachers

French Song Tracks

Danielle Robichaud – 'A quoi servent les lettres'

French lyrics with English translation – 'Alouette'

Alain Le Lait – 'Arc-en-ciel'

Alain Le Lait – 'Assis, debou'

Alain Le Lait – 'Bonjour!'

French Songs About Animals

Alain Le Lait – 'Avec un gros nez'

Danielle Robichaud avec Al Davis – 'Les animaux de la ferme' (farm animals)

Danielle Robichaud avec Al Davis – 'Les animaux du zoo' (zoo animals)

Alain Le Lait – 'Les poissons' (fish)

French Songs About Clothing, Weather, and Names of Parts of the Body

Alain Le Lait – 'Des os, il en faut'

Alain Le Lait – 'Drôle de tête'

Danielle Robichaud avec Al Davis – 'Les parties du corps' (body parts)

Danielle Robichaud avec Al Davis – 'Les saisons' (the seasons)

Teaching French Through Songs and Games – 'Savez-vous planter les choux?'

Danielle Robichaud avec Al Davis – 'Le temps' (the weather)

Danielle Robichaud avec Al Davis – 'Les vêtements' (clothes)

French Songs About Colours and Foods

Danielle Robichaud – '1, 2, 3, 4, carré'

Alain Le Lait – 'Ah, les légumes'

Danielle Robichaud avec Al Davis – 'Les couleurs' (colours)

Danielle Robichaud avec Al Davis – 'Les fruits' (fruits)

Danielle Robichaud avec Al Davis – 'Les légumes' (vegetables)

Alain Le Lait – 'Où as-tu mis les spaghettis?'

Numbers and Counting Fun in French

Danielle Robichaud avec Al Davis – 'Compter de 1 à 10' (counting from 1 to 10)

Teaching French Through Songs and Games – 'Mon merle a perdu une plume'

German Songs

'A, a, a, der Winter, der ist da' – A, a, a, Winter is Here

'Abel, Babel, Gänseschnabel' – Abel, Babel, Goose Bill
(ball bouncing song)

'Kommt ein Vogel geflogen' – A Bird Comes A-flying

'Ein Vogel wollte Hochzeit machen' – A Bird Wanted to
Get Married

'Auf einem Baum ein Kuckuck saß' – A Cuckoo Settled
on a Tree

'Eine kleine Geige' – A Little Violin

'Alle Meine Entchen' – All My Ducklings

'Alle Vögel sind schon da' – All the Birds Are Already
Here

'Und wer im Januar geboren ist' – And Who Was Born
in January

'Backe, backe Kuchen' – Bake, Bake the Cake

'Zwischen Berg und tiefem Tal' – Between Mountain and
Deep Valley

'Bruder Jacob – Brother James'

'Kinn Wippchen – Chin Tipping' (finger play)

'Komm, lieber Mai' – Come, Dear May

'Kommt ein Mann die Trepp heran' – A Man Comes Up
the Stairs (nursery rhyme)

'Kuckuck, Kuckuck' – Cuckoo, Cuckoo

'Tanz, Kindlein, tanz' – Dance, Little Child, Dance!
(children's song)

'Schneeflöckchen, Weißröckchen' – Dancing Snow-flakes,
White-lace Flowers (A traditional German Carol)

'Liebe Schwester, tanz mit mir' – Dear Sister, Dance
   With Me!
'Ich bin ein Musikante' – I Am a Musician (folk song)
'Wenn ich ein Vöglein wär' – If I Were a Little Bird
'Ich geh mit meiner Laterne 2' – I Go with My Lantern
   (St Martin's Day song, long version)

Spanish Songs for Teachers

Songs that Teach the Alphabet in Spanish
'Alfabeto' – Early Spanish Adventures
'¿Saben los sonidos de las letras?' – Jim Rule

Spanish Songs for Teaching Animal Names

'Con una nariz muy grande' – Seamos Amigos
'En la granja' (rap) – Étienne
'Jungle Safari Animales' – Early Spanish Adventures
'La ranita' – Jim Rule
'Sí, yo puedo / Yes I Can' – Jody Dreher

Counting with Numbers in Spanish Songs

'Diez niños / Ten Children' – Sing Your Way to Spanish

Songs to improve Dyslexia, Dyspraxia and Oral Communication

Alice Cooper – 'School's Out'
Chuck Berry – 'School Days'
Paul Simon – 'The Teacher'
The Beach Boys – 'Be True to Your School'
Gary U.S. Bonds – 'No More Homework'
Bobby McFerrin – 'Don't Worry Be Happy'

The Pointer Sisters – 'Yes, We Can Can'
The Beach Boys – 'Fun, Fun, Fun'
Patti LaBelle – 'New Attitude'
Gloria Esteffan and the Miami Sound Machine – '1-2-3'
The Monotones – 'Book of Love'
Bill Hayley and The Comets – 'Rock Around the Clock'
The Bangles – 'Manic Monday'
The Isley Brothers – 'Shout'
Manfred Mann – 'Do Wah Diddy Diddy'
The Coasters – 'Yakety Yak'
Danny and the Juniors – 'At the Hop'
Bobby Darin – 'Splish Splash'

REMEMBER

 *Sound Waves Make Brain Waves* with Language when you:

- Choose the right extracts using 80–120 BPM.

- Use the music to learn key vocabulary or the language itself.

- Use different music for different purposes, to set the scene of learning.

- Sing songs for languages as well as songs to help speech difficulties.

- Share the name of the extract with the pupils.

Smart Study

Study Skills and Revision

For some pupils, individual study can be one of the most challenging aspects of learning. One reason for this is they simply have not learned – or have not been taught – the best way for studying and revising, and this problem can be as challenging as getting to grips with the subject content itself. In many schools, pupils are still not shown how to study and learn, and Study Skills has become a Cinderella subject. Part of the teacher's role is to guide, support and coach pupils as they learn how best to analyse, learn, recall and memorise the information they encounter. One thing this *Little Book* offers, which you can use to support study and enhance revisions skills, is how to use appropriate music for the specific type of study and revision.

Some learners find it difficult to pick out the key points, to see the patterns and to form generalisations – which could be described as 'meta-cognition'. Instead, they try too hard to rote learn and internalise as much information as possible. You may have seen them highlighting almost everything on the page! Knowing what's important is a learnable skill, which can be enhanced with the right music playing. Given an extensive exposure to the use of music as a learning aid, the pupils will develop their own musical catalogues for Study and Revision Music. They will have learned what works for them in terms of the right music for doing a specific activity. Over time, each pupil will become more aware of how their memories, emotions, states of mind, and facility in communicating, have developed, and this increase in self-confidence will assist them in working on their own. Then 'Homework Becomes Own Work' and something to be proud of.

With the music, learning becomes an enjoyable exercise. Knowing what to pay attention to, and what to do with it, becomes simpler. And using all the senses to learn and then revise makes for more efficient recall and understanding later.

The first step for the teacher is to show and share with the learner ways of developing appropriate, and supportive, study and revision skills with the right music for the right task.

What do I need to do?

- Share study skills tricks with the learners. If it is appropriate, you can offer them a Study/Revision Diary. Better still, get the learners to create their own. They could even negotiate sharing their information and techniques with each other.

- Explain to the learners that there are two aspects of using the music tracks. First, they link the music to whatever it is they are learning, and then the same music can be used to help them with recall.

- Clarify the learning objectives of the task: explain what you want the learners to do and how you want them to approach the task. They may need specific guidance on how they listen, what to pay attention to. They also need to know whether you want them to work individually or with another learner.

• Never use a musical extract which has lyrics/words when employing this way of working, because the learner will experience a 'dual task paradigm' and – may focus on the lyrics rather than the presented text, thus confusing the content of the lyric with the content of the information being studied.

How to do this in the classroom

Listening Stage 1

• Explain clearly what you want the pupils to study/ revise. (Provide the information at this point in any form you wish, e.g. handout, worksheet, diary, computer etc.)

• Play the music and watch the learners, ensuring they are engrossed in the music.

• Start them working on the material they need to study or revise.

Listening Stage 2

• When you choose to finish playing the musical extract, get the learners to present the information in a format which is easy for them to remember. They could use mindmapping, draw spider diagrams, make bullet point lists and so on. Using different colours, drawing pictures, enhances the process.

- They will then revise the same material again with the same extract of music. Because they have made the links with the particular piece of music, they are far more likely to *remember, recall* and *understand* what they were expected to learn.

- Play the music again at the end of the lesson (with the volume level set on 'low') and get the learner to either *speak, share* or *show* to another learner or to you. (Some may choose to continue revising and studying individually. It is important to honour each student's preferred method of recall.)

Listening Stage 3

- You can test a pupil's ability to recall what they have learned by using some kind of assessment procedure. During the testing stage, play the same music quietly in the background.

- If continued revision and recall of the learning is necessary, offer the name of the musical extract and where the learner could get it for free.

- Make sure you note the date, time and task presented with this extract, to avoid playing the same extract again with different information, as the learners will become confused, and all that they have been learning and recalling will be transformed into gobbledygook!

Suggested Musical Extracts for Study Skills and Revision

These extracts are suitable because of their musical shape and average between 80–120 BPM. The frequencies support memory skills and, following the beats and changes in musical timbre, sound pulses create alpha waves which help the learner concentrate.

Adolph Adam – 'Valse' from *Giselle*

Edmund Angerer – 'Toy Symphony'

David Arkenstone – 'In the Wake of the Wind'

J. S. Bach – 'Suites for Orchestra 1-4': BWV 1066-69

Beethoven – 'Egmont Overture'

Beethoven – 'Piano Concerto No. 5': Opus 73

Geoffrey Burgon – Soundtrack from *Brideshead Revisited*: 'Julia'

Geoffrey Burgon – Soundtrack from *Brideshead Revisited*: 'Sebastian Against the World'

Geoffrey Burgon – Soundtrack from *Brideshead Revisited*: 'The Hunt'

Debussy – 'La Mer'

Debussy – 'Claire de Lune'

Disney – Selection from the film *Fantasia*

Fauré – 'Pavane': Modern version from *Utopia*

Jean Michel Jarre – 'Oxygene 2'

Robert Miles – 'Dreamland': 'Children'

Mozart – 'Piano Concerto No. 27 in B-Flat Major K595'

Mozart – 'Serenade in D Major': Mvt 1

Mozart – 'Divertimento in D Major'

Chapter 1: Music for Learning, Memory and Focus

Mozart – 'Serenade in D Major': Mvt 3

Mozart – 'Violin Concerto No. 3': Adagio

Mozart – 'Adagio for Violin and Orchestra'

Mozart – 'Eine Kleine Nachtmusik': Allegro

Mozart – 'Symphony No. 35': Mvt 3

Robert Prizeman – 'Libera': 'Mysterium'

Schubert – 'Rosamunde'

Soundtrack – *A.I.*: 'Where Dreams Are Born'

J. Strauss – 'Blue Danube': Waltz

R. Strauss – 'Also Sprach Zarathustra': Theme from *2001: A Space Odyssey*

Sweet Harmony – 'The Beloved': Live the Dream Mix (instrumental)

Tchaikovsky – 'Swan Lake': Waltz

Vivaldi – 'Flute Concerto in D': Allegro

Vivaldi – 'Concerto in C Major for 2 Trumpets'

John Williams – Soundtrack from *Schindler's List*: 'Theme from Schindler's List'

John Williams – Soundtrack from *A.I.*: 'Where Dreams are Born'

Hans Zimmer – Soundtrack from *Gladiator*: 'Now We Are Free'

REMEMBER

 *Sound Waves Make Brain Waves* with Study Skills and Revision when you:

- Choose the right extracts which have a tempo of 80–120 BPM.

- Present what you want studied and revised.

- Play the music whilst pupils are studying and revising, as they will make learning links between the information and the music.

- Do not use lyrics if they are presenting the problem through words.

- Share the name of the extract with the pupils and remind them that the right *Sound Waves Make Brain Waves*.

- Ask the pupils at a later stage what type of techniques they have developed with the music to help them study/revise.

Chapter 2:
Music for Relaxation and Calm

Overview

The ancient Greeks used music to calm the behaviour of belligerent drunks and as a 'medicine' for those who displayed unacceptable behaviour. In more recent times, Tyne and Wear Metro, drawing on a study in Canada in 2005, began playing classical music through speakers to disperse gangs of youngsters at Tynemouth, Whitley Bay and Cullercoats stations. Meanwhile, the London Underground has also flirted with the idea and has been running a pilot project at Elm Park station on the District Line in East London, apparently with some success. Relaxing music can quiet your nerves and free the flow of pleasant dream-like thoughts. Studies, from the United States to Shanghai, show that listening to music promotes interaction and a sense of communal well-being, and that individuals direct their thoughts in a more focused way when music is playing in the background[2].

Music makes people more likely to say what they feel[3] and it has been shown to induce significant improvements in relaxation, better moods, and happier thoughts, even amongst learners with Emotional and Behavioural Difficulties (EBD) . Relaxing music can break down barriers and create shared social space through sound waves. It can also help control social situations, to keep everyone feeling friendly and satisfied.

We live in a hectic and chaotic society which often seems overwhelming, given the amount of work and the number of daily jobs we are expected to carry out. Music can be used as a counterbalancing, inward-directed experience, and in a learning environment it will pull your pupils into their own sonic space, filtering out the noises and distractions that inevitably cause chaos at times. Using music will free the learners' consciousness from external concerns and help them relax at a deep, inner level.

This chapter will support learning and emotional responses to tasks and activities in the classroom for yourself and your learners. You will discover how Music for Hooking-Up, Calming Down and Chilling Out will get the learners ready for your lesson, and that Cleansing, Inner-Discipline and the Power of Headphones will be the specific application of music for behaviour, whilst music for Setting the Scene can be used to set the tone of the lesson or task. And my favourite, Music for Visualisation and Creation, will set free the creativity of all learners and develop creative thinking skills.

Now that you are familiar with the processes of applying the tool of music in your classroom, this chapter will feel easy to apply and should also have an effect on you as the teacher/facilitator of learning. Remember, this *Little Book* is not just a resource tool but a book of motivation ideas to develop your own catalogues of music for learning and life. The right music at the right time, linked with the application of *Sound Waves Make Brain Waves*, will most definitely make you feel relaxed and calm.

Music for Hooking Up,

Calming Down and Chilling Out

Music for relaxation and calm can help you and your learners cope effectively with stress and anxiety. You'll be better able to deal with impatience, people problems, panic, lack of balance, and dysfunctional behaviour. It's also good for getting ready for learning, for moving from one lesson to another, for meditation, and for sleep. Above all, it will save you from the ravages of tension.

Relaxing music flows through your nervous system to counteract the effects of stress on your body. In your mind, the right kinds of music can stimulate alpha Brain Waves for clear thinking and patience, or delta waves that signal sleep. When tension gets the upper hand and panic sets in, music can interrupt the negative biofeedback loop between the mind and body. On the interpersonal front, relaxing music has been shown to promote communication among people, easing difficult discussions and averting potential confrontations (remember how some of my own students used music to help calm down arguing parents).

Musical extracts can change or affect the way that you and your learners approach a task, become calm and focused for the beginning of a lesson, and even bring the learners back down from an exciting and thrilling lesson or a hectic lunchtime. For teachers who like to use *Brain Gym*® exercises, you can combine the music with the Hook-Up strategy. Follow these prompts to initiate the Hook-Up method:

• First, get the learners to place both arms in front of them with the palms of their hands open and facing outwards.

• Keeping the palms of their hands open, get them to cross one arm over the other then (in a cross position) link their fingers together like a basket weave.

• When the fingers are woven and crossed, turn the arm upwards towards the chest, like an inside-out movement.

• Rest the cross-woven arms and hands in the centre of the chest and relax. Do not bring the arms up too high up as this will be very uncomfortable.

Many teachers have found that combining music with the Hook-Ups is a really powerful way of relaxing the mind and body and getting the students ready for learning.

How to do this in the classroom

Listening Stage 1

- Explain and demonstrate the Hook-Up technique. You will only need to do this once, as the learners will know what you mean when you say 'Into Hook-Ups' the next time. Stand in the Hook-Up position yourself.

- Choose your extract carefully from the suggested list. Explain the *Sound Waves Make Brain Waves* notion and the reasons behind using music for relaxation and calm, and that you need the learners to close their eyes. This will help them to listen better and to be inside their own personal music bubble.

- Ask the learners to make themselves comfortable in the Hook-Up position but insist that they close their eyes to listen to the music.

- Begin to play the music quietly and let the music do the rest. (In future lessons, once you indicate the Hook-Up position the learners will know what to do and this means you can have the music playing quietly as they enter the room, or at any other point during the lesson.)

- Raise or lower the volume of the music depending on the strength of impact you wish to achieve. Remember that if the music is too loud it may cause some discomfort.

Listening Stage 2

- Play the music for a minimum of two minutes. The lengths of the suggested tracks are fine. You will become more familiar with their application as you become more confident in their usage.

- Pupils should be ready for learning by the time you finish playing the musical extract. I always say, 'Now we are ready for learning.' This will re-enforce the *Sound Waves Make Brain Waves* idea.

Listening Stage 3

- Make a note of the track. You may choose to use this track again if the learners become familiar with the fact that it is linked to Relaxation and Calm and Hook-Ups.

- Offer the name of the musical extract and where the learner could get it from if they choose to use it themselves in their homes.

Suggested musical extracts to use for Relaxation and Calm

The extracts are chosen because they will reduce heart rate, calm individuals, and set a relaxation tone to the classroom and individual learners. An average of 60–80 BPM will create Delta Waves, the electrical frequencies of sleep, which will slow the learners down and get them totally relaxed – but not actually asleep!

 ### *Music for Behaviour, Hook-Ups, Ready to Learn*

Samuel Barber – 'Adagio for Strings'

Ennio Morricone – Soundtrack from *The Mission*: 'On Earth as It Is in Heaven'

Ennio Morricone – Soundtrack from *The Mission*: 'Falls'

Ennio Morricone – Soundtrack from *The Mission*: 'Gabriel's Oboe'

Ennio Morricone – Soundtrack from *The Mission*: 'Brothers'

Karl Jenkins – 'Adiemus': from 'Adiemus Live'

Karl Jenkins – 'Cantus Insolitus': from 'Adiemus Live'

Karl Jenkins – 'The Wooing of Etain': from 'Adiemus Live'

Karl Jenkins – 'Dawn Dancing'

Libera – 'Salva Me'

Libera – 'Sanctus'

Libera – 'Agnus Dei'

Libera – 'Mysterium'

Hans Zimmer – Soundtrack from *Gladiator*: 'Now We Are Free'

Michael Nyman – Soundtrack from *The Piano*: 'The Heart Asks Pleasure'

Leon – 'Libera Me'

Geoffrey Burgon – Soundtrack from *Brideshead Revisited*: 'Julia's Theme'

Geoffrey Burgon – Soundtrack from *Brideshead Revisited*: 'Orphans of the Storm'

Geoffrey Burgon – Soundtrack from *Brideshead Revisited*: 'Sebastian Alone'

Geoffrey Burgon – Soundtrack from *Brideshead Revisited*: 'Venice Nocturne'

Music and Albums for Relaxation and Calm

Kitaro – 'Mandala'

Steven Halpern – 'Serenity Suite': 'Music and Nature'

Enya – 'Paint the Sky and Stars'

Paul Winter – 'Common Ground'

Ray Lynch – 'Deep Breakfast'

Hisham – 'Somewhere in a Dream'

Georgia Kelly – 'Seapeace'

Harry Pickens – 'Peace and Quiet'

Anastasi – 'CinemOcean'

Yanni – 'Devotion – The Best of Yanni'

Chopin – 'The Complete Nocturnes'

Debussy – 'La Mer'

Daniel Kobialka – 'Oh, What a Beautiful Morning'

John Surman – 'Coruscating'

Dial & Oatts – 'Between Us & Harmonic' from the Stringworks Album.

REMEMBER

 *Sound Waves Make Brain Waves* with Hook Ups when you:

- Explain and demonstrate how to do Hook-Ups.

- Choose a suitable extract from the list which uses 60–80 BPM.

- Ask the students to close their eyes when listening to the music.

- Say, 'Ready for learning' when the music finishes, as the pupils will be relaxed and focused.

You can use this strategy at any point during the lesson to switch between activities, or just use at the beginning or end of lessons.

Cleansing, Inner-Discipline and the Power of Headphones

Do you ever find yourself struggling to get your learners to be calm when you personally feel as if you are ready to explode? Music can help. Aristotle referred to music as medicine because of its cathartic powers. This is something you can utilise in your classroom to help students deal with unwanted emotions. Try using music to vent your own anger, frustration and grief, as well as the anger, frustration and bad behaviour that may be displayed or suppressed by some of your class.

Much has been written and spoken about the supposed connection between 'hard-core' music styles and aggressive or violent behaviours[4]. While such debate is important, it often overlooks the fact that stormy, turbulent music has been composed throughout the world for centuries. Listening to a variety of music from 'Beethoven's Fifth' to the explosive vocalising Kecak of Bali, it is not possible to attribute any causal link between hard-core music and societies of violence. It is more useful to consider that people make music to serve vital personal and social purposes.

Some research has proposed that music such as heavy metal, rock and hard-core rap leads to aggression, violence and often drug abuse. Findings suggest that exposure to violent media images correlates with behaviour and attitude problems, particularly amongst adolescent males.

However, none of these investigations found that listening to turbulent music actually leads to aggressive or self-destructive behaviour. It seems more likely that angry, at-risk people have a preference for 'negative' music, which they use not as a healthy catharsis but as affirmation of their troubled state. Furthermore, many controlled studies that link music to an undesirable effect or behaviour have supplemented the music with strong visual images. These results, then, don't describe the effect music has on people, but rather testify to the way music has been appended to television, movie and video images to heighten the emotional experience of visual events.

Many of the learners in your classroom will at some point display moments of anger, frustration or grief. The message here is to make sure you do not increase the intensity of these behaviours by shouting or raising your voice in order to get the students focused. Instead, choose and use music to calm down individuals and groups and to help them achieve a more focused, forward-thinking state of mind.

For this purpose I advocate the use of personal headphones for anyone who displays behaviour which is affecting not only their own work but also that of others. If the majority of the class is focused and ready for learning, then you can ask those who are not ready to move themselves into a quiet personal zone. They can do this when they realise – or you tell them – that their behaviour is out of control. The combination of the right music and headphones with someone who has withdrawn from the main learning group will support and help that person to regulate his or her own behaviour, and allow them to become more focused on the tasks and learning ahead.

This idea has been tried and tested; it works just about every time. After all, better the headphones than personal confrontation with you or the others in your class. Used correctly, this will be a calm and thought-provoking means to inclusive education without a learner taking advantage of the situation. After all, it's *your* music they are listening to, not their own!

So, let the use of headphones for some individuals be the key to better learning and behaviour. You can allow the 'positive' students to bring in their own listening tools, such as iPods and other MP3 players with their own head-phones. If they are banned in your school you can justify their correct use for learning specifically in your own classroom. With guidelines, ground rules, proper negotia-tions and the correct music, you will see standards of learning improve – and that's what you want, isn't it?

What do I need to do?

- Make sure you have equipment such as an MP3 player, iPod, CD player or computer, with a set of headphones.

- Have available suitable music tracks for the individual, or if possible let the learner download the tracks you intend to use onto their own players. It does work – trust me!

- Tell the learner which track you want them to listen to, or if they are old enough, the appropriate track can be chosen by them.

- Make sure you tell the individual it is 'quiet time' and that no interruptions are permitted at any point.

- Set an appropriate time for calming down. When a track has been listened to, re-integrate the learner. You could also get them to use the Hook-Up technique here.

Some teachers worry about students misbehaving just so that they can listen to music. In my own classroom I use music with learners who have Emotional and Behavioural Difficulties (EBD), and this is usually accepted by the rest of the class as a 'teacher strategy' to support that individual. There are occasions when I have to use this technique with other learners, but they understand this is for discipline purposes.

How to do this in the classroom

Listening Stage 1

- Ensure the learner is comfortable and in an area that is non-threatening, private and safe for the individual or others.

- Explain the reason for their withdrawal from the main learning group, and that they will have some quiet time using music to support their individual behaviour.

- Select the track you want the pupil to listen to and, if appropriate, suggest they use the Hook-Up technique.

- When the music track has finished, choose an appropriate time for re-entry into the learning area. Make it clear this is not a reward but a tool to address the aggression and frustration that is not only affecting the learner's own work but the work of others as well.

I find the clear and concise explanation of *Sound Waves Make Brain Waves* supports the management strategy for using music to calm or pre-empt difficult situations in the classroom. It is a positive consequence – instead of having a disaffected learner or one who disrupts others you have used music as a management tool, demonstrating your ability to create and maintain a positive classroom led by a positive classroom teacher. Believe me it works!

Listening Stage 2

- Make a note of the track. You may want to use it again if the learner has had a positive experience and it has helped with behaviour.

- Offer the name of the musical extract and where the learner could get it from if they choose to use it in the home. After all, it is not just in school where learners become aggressive and frustrated and demonstrate unacceptable behaviour.

- Let the learner continue using these tracks at home and offer the opportunity of keeping an Aggression Log or Headphone Healing Book. If the learner has special needs, or is receiving specific support for behaviour and learning, then this would support future review sessions and IEPs (Individual Education Plans).

- Explain that *Sound Waves Make Brain Waves* by playing different types of music. This chapter relates to the individual learner who demonstrates EBD.

Suggested Musical Extracts to Use for Relaxation and Calm

The extracts are chosen because they will reduce heart rate, calm the individual and help with behaviour, they will induce Delta Waves to enable the learner to become fully relaxed. Pieces are 60-80 BPM.

 ### *Music for Cleansing Behaviour – Headphone Power*

Samuel Barber – 'Adagio for Strings'

Ennio Morricone – Soundtrack from *The Mission*: 'On Earth as It Is in Heaven'

Ennio Morricone – Soundtrack from *The Mission*: 'Falls'

Ennio Morricone – Soundtrack from *The Mission*: 'Gabriel's Oboe'

Ennio Morricone – Soundtrack from *The Mission*: 'Brothers'

Karl Jenkins – 'Adiemus': from 'Adiemus Live'

Karl Jenkins – 'Cantus Insolitus': from 'Adiemus Live'

Karl Jenkins – 'The Wooing of Etain': from 'Adiemus Live'

Karl Jenkins – 'Dawn Dancing'

Libera – 'Salva Me'

Libera – 'Sanctus'

Libera – 'Agnus Dei'

Libera – 'Mysterium'

Hans Zimmer – Soundtrack from *Gladiator*: 'Now We Are Free'

Michael Nyman – Soundtrack from *The Piano*: 'The Heart Asks Pleasure'

Leon – 'Libera Me'

Geoffrey Burgon – Soundtrack from *Brideshead Revisited*: 'Julia's Theme'

Geoffrey Burgon – Soundtrack from *Brideshead Revisited*: 'Orphans of the Storm'

Geoffrey Burgon – Soundtrack from *Brideshead Revisited*: 'Sebastian Alone'

Geoffrey Burgon – Soundtrack from *Brideshead Revisited*: 'Venice Nocturne'

Music and Albums for Relaxation and Calm

Kitaro – 'Mandala'

Steven Halpern – 'Serenity Suite': 'Music and Nature'

Enya – 'Paint the Sky and Stars'

Paul Winter – 'Common Ground'

Ray Lynch – 'Deep Breakfast'

Hisham – 'Somewhere in a Dream'

Georgia Kelly – 'Seapeace'

Harry Pickens – 'Peace and Quiet'

Anastasi – 'CinemOcean'

Yanni – 'Devotion – The Best of Yanni'

Chopin – 'The Complete Nocturnes'
Debussy – 'La Mer'
Daniel Kobialka – 'Oh, What a Beautiful Morning'
John Surman – 'Coruscating'
Dial & Oatts – 'Between Us & Harmonic'

REMEMBER

 *Sound Waves Make Brain Waves* for cleansing and inner-discipline when you:

- Choose a suitable extract from the list which uses 60–80 BPM.

- Ensure a suitable player and headphones are to hand.

- Give the student the track to listen to.

- Set the student the amount of time as 'quiet time'.

- Allow the student to use the hook-up technique if required.

- Say, 'Ready for learning' when the music finishes, as the pupils will be relaxed and focused.

Setting the Scene

In the previous chapter I mentioned using the 'Hook-Up' technique to affect or change the behaviour of individual learners, to bring them down, and to change their emotional make-up. You can also use extracts of music to set the scene for learning and thinking as students enter the room, or when you want to change the nature of the task or activity. You could think of this as 'changing the emotional wallpaper' of the classroom. This is probably one of the easiest ways to begin using music in your classroom, especially if you are still learning about the more complex application of 'the right music at the right time' scenario.

If you're working on a particularly poignant or emotional task, music is your tool. Music affects the emotions and may even provoke a physical response. Choose your pieces carefully here so that you can link the activity with the mood that the music creates. You can also use excerpts of music other than those on the suggested list, especially if some of the learners themselves listen to music which they feel calms their minds and bodies ready for deep thought and reflection. The right music to create the right mood or scene is the key here. It might be music directly linked to the task, music to set a mood, or even an extract with appropriate lyrics – this is what I call music for setting the scene. This is the part of using music where you do not need to explain to the learners beforehand why you are using or playing the music – although it can be a useful exercise to ask them afterwards if they felt the music made a difference to them.

How to do this in the classroom

Listening Stage 1

- Listen to some of the suggested extracts yourself and choose at least five which have a very calming effect on you, or even those pieces that have appropriate lyrics for setting the scene. If the music works for you, then it may do it for the learners. Select one to use.

- Begin to play the music quietly as they enter the room, making sure the volume level is not too loud. This will set the scene and begin 'papering the learning walls' with soothing sounds

- When seated, the learners can close their eyes if they wish to. Having their eyes closed will help them immerse themselves in the sound waves around the room.

- Watch the learners as they listen. Scan the room for physical changes as you see the students relaxing and becoming ready for learning.

- Different extracts of music will change the learning wallpaper in different ways. The softer the music, the softer the response. The more colourful the music, the more vibrant the wallpaper. Let the music run for a minimum of two minutes, but the lengths of the suggested tracks are fine. You will become more familiar with their application and the times needed as you use music more in your classroom. Setting the right tone for the lesson is crucial and the scene will be set for learning.

Listening Stage 2

• In my experience, many learners choose to listen to the extracts used in class when doing their homework. This helps them get in the mood.

• Make a note of the track – you may choose to use it again if the learners become familiar with the fact that it is linked to Relaxation and Calm, and Setting the Scene, in which ever way you choose to use it.

• Offer the name of the musical extract and where the learners could get it for free. Give the pupils a handout of the extracts that you have used or choose to use in future. You will be surprised that even the most unlikely learners whom you would never expect to listen to this type of music will become thrilled by the effects.

Suggested Musical Extracts to Use for Relaxation and Calm

The extracts are chosen because they are excellent to set a scene for a lesson or change the emotional make-up of the classroom or task. This is linked with the subtle textures and timbres of the instrumentation and tempo. They emulate a very slow heart rate and create a relaxed atmosphere and have a tempo of 60–90 BPM.

Music for Setting the Scene

Samuel Barber – 'Adagio for Strings'

Ennio Morricone – Soundtrack from *The Mission*: 'On Earth as It Is in Heaven'

Ennio Morricone – Soundtrack from *The Mission*: 'Falls'

Ennio Morricone – Soundtrack from *The Mission*: 'Gabriel's Oboe'

Ennio Morricone – Soundtrack from *The Mission*: 'Brothers'

Karl Jenkins – 'Adiemus': 'Adiemus Live'

Karl Jenkins – 'Cantus Insolitus': from 'Adiemus Live'

Karl Jenkins – 'The Wooing of Etain': from 'Adiemus Live'

Karl Jenkins – 'Dawn Dancing'

Libera – 'Salva Me'

Libera – 'Sanctus'

Libera – 'Agnus Dei'

Libera – 'Mysterium'

Hans Zimmer – Soundtrack from *Gladiator*: 'Now We Are Free'

Michael Nyman – Soundtrack from *The Piano*: 'The Heart Asks Pleasure'

Leon – 'Libera Me'

Geoffrey Burgon – Soundtrack from *Brideshead Revisited*: 'Julia's Theme'

Geoffrey Burgon – Soundtrack from *Brideshead Revisited*: 'Orphans of the Storm'

Geoffrey Burgon – Soundtrack from *Brideshead Revisited*: 'Sebastian Alone'

Geoffrey Burgon – Soundtrack from *Brideshead Revisited*:
  'Venice Nocturne'

Music and Albums for Relaxation and Calm

Kitaro – 'Mandala'
Steven Halpern – 'Serenity Suite': 'Music and Nature'
Enya – 'Paint the Sky and Stars'
Paul Winter – 'Common Ground'
Ray Lynch – 'Deep Breakfast'
Hisham – 'Somewhere in a Dream'
Georgia Kelly – 'Seapeace'
Harry Pickens – 'Peace and Quiet'
Anastasi – 'CinemOcean'
Yanni – 'Devotion – The Best of Yanni'
Chopin – 'The Complete Nocturnes'
Debussy – 'La Mer'
Daniel Kobialka – 'Oh, What a Beautiful Morning'
John Surman – 'Coruscating'
Dial & Oattis – 'Between Us and Harmonic'

REMEMBER

 *Sound Waves Make Brain Waves* with Setting the Scene when you:

- Create an atmosphere appropriate for your teaching needs.

- Use the correct extracts, with or without lyrics, in order to get the learners ready and focused. This music should have a tempo of 60–90 BPM.

- Check the volume level is not too loud! This is important.

- Music can be played at *any* time during the lesson if you want to change or set the scene for a different purpose.

- This type of music can also calm learners. Get them to close their eyes, as it helps them to immerse themselves in the Sound Waves.

Visualisation and Creation – Hear It, See It

Music has a vital role to play in the current climate of educational change, with the strong emphasis on creativity and thinking skills. Creativity isn't just about generating ideas, it is also about making them happen. For Michelangelo, just imagining the Sistine Chapel wasn't enough – he had to paint it too! Experimental evidence suggests that listening to music enhances people's creativity – probably an unsurprising discovery, but one whose potential remains largely untapped.

With this in mind, many teachers are using music to help learners visualise scenes for artwork, poetry, creative writing or drama. The mind is a wonderful tool for creating mental pictures, as the learners fantasise about what could be. Many of these experiences have a dream-like quality; however, with the correct direction in your teaching, students convert these states of fantasy to something more realistic by bringing their visualisations to life in the form of pictures, words, movements or musical compositions. So many teachers are now using these techniques to support the learner with creative flow that it has become one of the most popular ways of addressing the creative thinking process. Imagination is a wonderful thing!

The primary purpose of this chapter is to suggest ways in which you can use music as a tool for developing imagery and visualisation. You can use the power of music to help your students create mental representations of a given scene or series of scenes. Sometimes these will be created with you leading them; at other times the learners will create these images themselves with the aid of music. Some pupils have reported that they cannot create mental pictures but instead experience a series of emotional changes. If this is the case, then you will need to ask them to describe their feelings or connections made with the music. Visualisations and guided imagery are very effective when used with the suggested extracts below.

Evidence from my own students suggest that certain types or pieces of music can create similar types of visual imagery as well as similar types of feelings, regardless of the listener! A case in point is 'Gabriel's Oboe' (from *The Mission*) which has prompted similar types of visualisations and changes in emotional state for a variety of listener-learners, from as young as five to adults of 75+. Amazingly, they have all reported the following:

Visualisations

- Running water, seascapes, lakes and rivers

- Beaches, warm sun

- Long paths through woodland

- A never-ending beach scene

- Angelic voices and clouds

- Weddings and happiness

- Floatation above the ground being able to see the world beneath

- Magic carpets, flying like a bird above the clouds

Emotional Changes

- Tears of joy and happiness

- Sense of release and well-being

- Total calm and tranquil moments

- Freedom and the ability to do anything

- Confidence in their abilities and a belief in themselves

These are the common experiences from thousands of listeners who have been exposed to 'Gabriel's Oboe', and every time it is played to a different audience they all share similar evocative visualisations or emotional changes. Now if that isn't proof that music makes connections with our emotional make-up and ability to create different scenes in our minds, then what is?

What do I need to do?

- Before playing the music decide the main focus of the task and whether or not you will be giving the learners some guided imagery at the beginning. For example:

  'You see your grandmother walking alone in the woods but she is too far for you to call to her. You move in the same direction and ...'

- If you are using the music purely to evoke creative visualisations and you want to get the learners to share these on paper, then make it clear that what they see in their minds when listening to the music is what you want to see on paper – be it in art form or creative writing etc.

- For those students who say they cannot see or experience a mental image, give them the opportunity to write their experiences on paper or tell you orally. You can record the storytelling and use it for a future task where the learner's experiences can be used as a starting point for further creative writing.

How to do this in the classroom

Listening Stage 1

- Ensure the learners are comfortable and the scene is set. Explain the task in detail and then initiate the music.

- Firstly, play the music and just listen, immersing the class in the wonderful sounds, textures and timbres of the extract. Tell them they are going on a journey of creativity and that you hope they will discover and experience wonderful emotions and visualisations whilst the music is playing.

- While playing the music, watch the learners. Scan the room for physical changes as you see them relaxing and enjoying the sounds echoing around the room. Play the music for a minimum of two to four minutes, but the lengths of the suggested tracks are fine. You will become more confident with their application the more you use them.

- When the music is finished ask the learners to open their eyes slowly and to continue to enjoy their experiences. Do not get them to speak to you at this point as you do not want to spoil the moment or interrupt the continued images or feelings which will remain in the students' minds and bodies.

Listening Stage 2

- Then play the music for a second time and let the learners share with you their experiences through drawing, painting, words and pictures, or even dramatic movements.

- Let them carry out the task, expressing themselves in whatever format you have instructed. The second playing of the music supports the individual experiences from the first listening.

- Make a note of the track – you may choose to use this track again if the learner becomes familiar with the fact that it is linked to Visualisation and Creation.

- Offer the name of the musical extract and where the learner could get it from if they choose to use it themselves in their homes. Remember, you can give the pupils a handout of the extracts that you have used or choose to use in future.

- Let the learners continue these experiences by offering the opportunity of using music at home and keeping a Creative Diary or Thought Book.

Suggested Musical Extracts to Use for Relaxation and Calm

The extracts are chosen because they are able to stimulate wonderful emotions and fantastic visualisations in the mind. This is evident in the research Music and the Mind – see *The Big Book of Independent Thinking* – and they stimulate theta waves, which are associated with creativity and imagination. Extracts are 60–110BPM.

 ### *Music for Visualisation and Creation*

Samuel Barber – 'Adagio for Strings'
Ennio Morricone – Soundtrack from *The Mission*: 'On Earth as It Is in Heaven'
Ennio Morricone – Soundtrack from *The Mission*: 'Falls'
Ennio Morricone – Soundtrack from *The Mission*: 'Gabriel's Oboe'
Ennio Morricone – Soundtrack from *The Mission*: 'Brothers'
Karl Jenkins – 'Adiemus': from 'Adiemus Live'
Karl Jenkins – 'Cantus Insolitus': from 'Adiemus Live'
Karl Jenkins – 'The Wooing of Etain': from 'Adiemus Live'.
Karl Jenkins – 'Dawn Dancing'
Libera – 'Salva Me'
Libera – 'Sanctus'
Libera – 'Agnus Dei'
Libera – 'Mysterium'
Hans Zimmer – Soundtrack from *Gladiator*: 'Now We Are Free'

Michael Nyman – Soundtrack from *The Piano*: 'The Heart Asks Pleasure'

Leon – 'Libera Me'

Geoffrey Burgon – Soundtrack from *Brideshead Revisited*: 'Julia's Theme'

Geoffrey Burgon – Soundtrack from *Brideshead Revisited*: 'Orphans of the Storm'

Geoffrey Burgon – Soundtrack from *Brideshead Revisited*: 'Sebastian Alone'

Geoffrey Burgon – Soundtrack from *Brideshead Revisited*: 'Venice Nocturne'

Music and Albums for Relaxation and Calm

Visualisation and Creation

Kitaro – 'Mandala'

Steven Halpern – 'Serenity Suite': 'Music and Nature'

Enya – 'Paint the Sky and Stars'

Paul Winter – 'Common Ground'

Ray Lynch – 'Deep Breakfast'

Hisham – 'Somewhere in a Dream'

Georgia Kelly – 'Seapeace'

Harry Pickens – 'Peace and Quiet'

Anastasi – 'CinemOcean'

Yanni – 'Devotion – The Best of Yanni'

Chopin – 'The Complete Nocturnes'

Debussy – 'La Mer'

Daniel Kobialka – 'Oh, What a Beautiful Morning'

John Surman – 'Coruscating'

Dial & Oatts – 'Between Us & Harmonic' from the Album 'Stringworks'

REMEMBER

 *Sound Waves Make Brain Waves* with Visualisation and Creation when you:

Suggest extracts with a tempo of 60–110 BPM.

- Choose extracts which are musically powerful enough to change a person's emotions.

- Use the extracts suggested that can create mind visualisations or fantasy scenes.

- Play the extracts at an appropriate level – not too loud. Remember that the ambience of the room is important too.

- Allow the learners to express their feelings or their visual experiences in any way they wish, unless specifically directed by yourself.

- Play the extract a second time to strengthen the experiences.

Chapter 3:
Music to Motivate, Stimulate and Energise

Overview

Music is audio fuel for action! When the sound of stimulating music hits the air and your inner ear, your cochlea converts it into electrical energy, sending it into your brain. In short, the right kind of music electrifies your body. Music that motivates, stimulates and energises you can also produce beta waves in your brain – the electrical patterns of about thirteen to thirty cycles per second that help you with external events, make quick decisions, and solve immediate problems. It may be a basic craving to be more awake in body and mind that makes people prefer music that moves at a faster speed with higher pitches and brighter sounds. Musical extracts support learners and teachers in becoming more motivated in their work, stimulated and energised to learn and study.

As well as using music to aid learning, it is also a great way to make you and your students feel good about themselves. Lyrics can be just as powerful as purely instrumental sounds, and I recommend pieces that you can use to motivate, stimulate and energise learners, both in an out of the classroom. It's all about getting the mind, brain and body moving, not just in a motivational sense but in a physical sense, too.

Energise yourself and get that body and mind working with up-beat, thrilling music in 'Shaking Off That Monday Morning Feeling', followed by shaking and waking your classroom with 'Rock the Classroom', then celebrating all things great with 'What Have You Done Today To Make Yourself Feel Proud?' Too often in education we forget to celebrate what we have done well. We are always seeking the next thing rather than acknowledging what we have already achieved. So, don't just sit there, think about what you have done today that makes you feel good about yourself and be proud of it. There is so much music you can access for this that you, too, will be able to add to the suggested tracks, making sure of course that they are pieces with a that tempo of between 100–165 BPM.

By now you will have experienced three different areas of using music to support learning and life. Make yourself feel proud by getting hold of other tracks apart from the ones suggested.

Shaking Off That Monday Morning Feeling

(On Monday, Tuesday, Wednesday...)

When you need peak performance, music can arouse your body, stimulate your mind, and fill you with the energy of sound. Energising music can help wake you up, create specific emotional states in the audience at presentations and performances, as well as for negotiation and competitive learning. Lively music can recharge the brain, motivate people to exercise and attend to their physical well-being – and provide adrenaline thrills that will leave you feeling 'magical'.

Music can be the fuel for action and energy, positive thinking and creativity. Let's just call it the 'new chocolate'! When the sound of stimulating music hits your inner ear, your cochlea converts it into the most wonderful electrical energy and sends it into your brain – these electrical impulses travel through your cortex, down your spine, through the sinoatrial node (the pacemaker for your heart), and out into your muscles, arousing every element of your autonomic nervous system as they go. In short, the right kind of music literally electrifies your body.

Motivating, stimulating and energising music produces beta waves in your brain, the electrical patterns of about thirteen to thirty cycles per second, and are associated with the ability to make quick decisions and solve immediate problems. It may be, of course, a basic craving to be more awake in body and mind that makes people prefer music that moves at a faster speed with higher pitches and brighter sounds – all characteristics of energising music. Most of us enjoy an up-beat feeling: up-beat mood music is an effective and safe way to achieve this.

Music can ease the transition from sleep to the everyday world of work and learning. For some people, the world looks better when they wake up to their favourite music. When you need to be awake for Monday morning lessons, some really energising up-beat music can do the trick. Short, snappy music, often with great lyrics, combined with your own willingness to move to the music, will motivate you and your students to be ready for learning. This is a tactic that works at any time.

My favourite morning wake-up song is 'C'mon Everybody' by Eddie Cochran. Assisted by the correct tracks, you should be able to stimulate the learners' minds and bodies and get rid of those morning blues.

Don't believe me? As an otherwise cynical science teacher once said to me:

'I started that Monday morning lesson with "C'mon Everybody". I told the kids to stand up and stand with me, clap when I clapped, dance when I danced and shout out … "C'mon Everybody!" when they needed to. Honestly, at the end of the session it was electric and the kids thought I had been mixing some chemicals in the back prep room!!! … but I didn't care … You should have seen their faces. I could see what they were thinking. Is she mad? Has she lost it? No … I'm here ready to teach and for you to learn. I now start every lesson with "C'mon Everybody" ... It's a must. I love it and the kids do too.'

What do I need to do?

- Be brave, be willing, get ready.

- Listen to a number of the tracks to get the feel of the music. Tap, clap and move to the music yourself before trying it with your class. Play them in the car, sing along, wind your window down and even sing to the rest of the world – at least it will be better than the free *Ibiza Uncovered* music you get when you're at a set of traffic lights!

- Remember: most teachers can act and stand on a stage, because that's what we do every day. This is just another aspect of that same process.

- Believe me, once you start using music with strong lyrics and drum beats your learners will never forget these high energy, high impact lessons. The 150–165 BPM music will excite the body and will have electrifying results.

How to do this in the classroom

Listening Stage 1

- Explain to the learners how they are going to be involved: it's OK to let go and be stimulated by songs, powerful beats and exciting timbres and textures.

- Play the music loudly so it fills the room. Get the class to face you and allow them to have a little space to move. When the piece is finished, relax and allow the students to express themselves with movement also – this is for any age. This will get rid of those Wake-Up Blues.

'Get ready ... steady ... let's get ready to rumble. Move to the beat ... stamp your feet ... clap your hands ... sing or chant the lyrics' – lead your learners to the music. Anyone can do this – be free – feel energised.

• Give yourself and your students a minute or so before beginning the lesson. Start with an active task: they will be geared up for anything at this stage.

In my experience, this is where you can take risks with learning and try something new ... you know the things I mean. All those weird and wacky ideas you pick up from visiting Inset providers, and you have never had the guts to try. Go on ... do it! You will be amazed at how receptive the learners will be at this stage. The more you get them involved, the more they will experience the electrical energy from the sound waves.

Listening Stage 2

• Make a note of the track – you may choose to use this track again if your learners become familiar with the fact that it is linked to becoming motivated, stimulated and energised and is great Wake-Up Music.

• You can choose to play this music in a learning carousel, or learning break, to switch between tasks.

- Offer the name of the musical extract and where the learner could get it for free if they choose to use it themselves in their homes.

Suggested Musical Extracts to Use for Motivating, Stimulating and Energising.

The music in this chapter stimulates Beta Waves, which will get your learners focused, excited and up-beat. These extracts range from 125–165 BPM.

Music for Wake-Up Blues – those Monday morning feelings.

Eddie Murphy – 'I'm a Believer'
Baha Men – 'Best Years of Our lives'
Eddie Cochran – 'C'mon Everybody'
The Proclaimers – 'I'm on My Way'
Blue Suede – 'Hooked on a Feeling'
Chubby Checker – 'Let's Twist Again'
Reel 2 Reel – 'I Like to Move It'
Fenua – 'Tiki Dance'
The Pointer Sisters – 'Neutron Dance'
Michael Buffer – 'Let's Get Ready to Rumble'
Ritchie Valens – 'La Bamba'
Arrow – 'Hot, Hot, Hot'
Jerry Lee Lewis – 'Great Balls of Fire'
BTO – 'You Ain't Seen Nothing Yet'
Van Halen – 'Jump'
The Esquires – 'Get on Up'
Danny and the Juniors – 'At the Hop'

Little Eva – 'Locomotion'
Manfred Mann – 'Do Wah Diddy Diddy'
James Brown – 'I Feel Good'
Mary J. Blige – 'Be Happy'
Chic – 'Good Times'

REMEMBER

 *Sound Waves Make Brain Waves* with Wake-Up Music when you:

- Share your enthusiasm with your learners, allow them to feel free and move to the music.

- Learn and know your music – move to the beat yourself.

- Are brave and try new things – move and dance or clap and sing in your classroom.

- Sing or chant with the lyrics and don't be afraid of having fun yourself.

- Pick your own tracks – remember they need to be between 125–165 BPM.

Rock the Classroom!

Pump up the volume! Sound Waves are energy, and higher volumes actually send more electrical pulses per second into your brain. Turn up the music until it resonates through your body – but never listen to music at a level that causes pain or discomfort. Feel the music from your head, down through your body, waking up nerves and muscles all the way to your fingers and toes.

Upper frequencies penetrate directly to your arousal centres and this 'phasic arousal' could be stimulated by the barking of a dog, or a rapidly approaching sound – or magnificent music at 125–175 BPM. So emphasise the music's high end frequencies with the tone dial or equaliser on your music system. Get the balance right – power listening is focused listening, and paying attention to energising music arouses your system even more. Make the music the total experience of the moment. Let the musical beats fill the room and move you from within. Your learners will be pumped up and ready to go.

However, the energising benefits of music can fade with time, so have extra music on hand to fill unexpected delays, and enjoy the successful application of rocking the room and your students. Choose music that indicates 'success' as well as the ones suggested below. When a song helps the learners to succeed, use it again the next time to condition yourself and them to succeed at tasks. Make sure you are energised in your work, and that the students are focused in their studies, by having plenty of music available which will encourage a faster heart rate, thus increasing excitement and eagerness to learn.

Songs or pieces that have a tempo of more than 125–175 BPM will get your learners rocking and rolling, thinking, and applying themselves to the learning task. If you want to mix listening with group work, team up the groups with music: give each group its own individual piece of music to listen and relate to. This will energise them and get them raring to go in the way that sports managers inspire their teams.

Do you want better co-ordination from your learners, as well as greater endurance and deeper conditioning? You can entrain a person's muscles by matching the pace of their movement to the speed of the music, and this type of music can be played during a task. Don't use music with lyrics if they are problem solving, otherwise learners will experience something called a 'dual-task paradigm'. This is where the lyrics and the thought process could hamper any critical and analytical thinking.

So, by using the right Sound Waves you will create the right Brain Waves and your learners will be 'rocking and rolling' in the learning environment.

What do I need to do?

- Familiarise yourself with your selection of music, at 125 BPM or above. Choose to use the music at any point to energise the learners, increasing heart beats and energy levels.

- If you plan to link the mood of the music or the lyrics to a lesson, it is important to choose songs with lyrics that fit the occasion. e.g. 'We Will, We Will Rock You' or 'You Can Make It If You Try'.

- Playing the right music at the right time with high energy lyrics and fantastic rock rhythms and songs will rock your classroom beyond belief.

How to do this in the classroom

Listening Stage 1

- Begin to play the music loudly. Allow the learners to be immersed in the music, surrounded by the lyrics, the textures and timbres of the piece.

- Indicate to the class how long the music will be played for and how it best fits your learning intentions. Let them know that it's OK to let go and be stimulated by songs, powerful beats and inspiring timbres and textures.

- Now turn up the volume. Ready ... steady ... thrill rides are a-coming. Move to the beat ... stamp your feet ... clap your hands ... sing or rap the lyrics. When the piece is finished feel the excited energy of the room.

Listening Stage 2

- Make a note of the track – you may choose to use this track again if the learners become familiar with the fact that it is linked to becoming motivated, stimulated and energised.

- Offer the name of the musical extract and where the learner could get it for free if they choose to use it themselves.

Suggested Musical Extracts to Use for Motivating, Stimulating and Energising Learners.

 Music to pump up the volume and energise pupils for learning

These extracts are all 125–175 BPM and this will create beat waves which make you highly alert, increase your heart rate and ready for any challenge!

Queen – 'We Will Rock You'
Duran Duran – 'Hungry Like a Wolf'
Wham – 'Wake Me Up Before You Go-Go'
Cyndi Lauper – 'She Bop'
Dead or Alive – 'You Spin Me Round'
The Bangles – 'Walk Like an Egyptian'
Three Dog Night – 'Celebrate'
Madonna – 'Holiday'
Queen – 'We Are the Champions'
Kool and the Gang – 'Celebration'
Tina Turner – 'The Best'
Reel 2 Reel – 'I Like to Move It Move It'
Michael Buffer – 'Let's Get Ready to Rumble'
The Pointer Sisters – 'I'm So Excited'

Jerry Lee Lewis – 'Great Balls of Fire'
Devo – 'Whip It'
Arrow – 'Hot, Hot, Hot'
The Cars – 'Shake It Up'
James Brown – 'I Feel Good'
Argent – 'Hold Your Head Up'
Mary J. Blige – 'Be Happy'
Chic – 'Good Times'

REMEMBER

 *Sound Waves Make Brain Waves* with Rock the Classroom by:

- Using extracts of 125–175 BPM.

- Listening to the extracts and becoming familiar with the lyrics and musical textures.

- Allowing yourself to be a little daring with some extracts – think outside the normal learning box.

- Volume full on!

- Share the music with your learners and get the classroom rocking.

What Have You Heard Today to Make You Feel Proud?

Thrilling lyrics in a song are enough to motivate most of us. Have you ever done something wonderful and then felt totally great? The memory of the moment may stay with you forever, but the power of that moment could fade in a short time[5]. There are ways of reliving such moments. So how can you repeat it? How do you get back that wonderful feeling whenever and wherever you want it? Simple.

Using music can almost immediately take you back to that great feeling.

Use music in your learning environment to motivate, stimulate and energise learners to do well, try their best and even reflect upon a moment of glory. Heather Small's 'What have you done today to make yourself feel proud?' is a brilliant way of getting learners to think about personal achievements and progress made. Don't just use it in your classroom though. Use it in assemblies, corridors, achievement evenings … and even in your car on the way home from work. Try it – it works.

Thrilling experiences – brief moments of unexpected exhilaration – are similar to the effects music can have on you. You get them from climbing mountains, bungee jumping, roller coasters, adventurous movies and even erotic embraces! And yes, when you're listening to music and your hairs stand on end and you get that all over tingling feeling, then you know that music is making a difference. In fact, the existence of this musical rush has been acknowledged for centuries. The Arabs called it *tarab* – the unique state of ecstasy brought on only by music. In Middle Eastern culture, music performances are often accompanied by ecstatic moans from the audience.

The physiology of thrills is still only partly understood. However, one test measuring the thrills that people experience while listening to music came to the titillating conclusion that music can cause 'chills, shudders, tingling and tickling' in the upper spine, back of the neck, shoulders, lower spine and scalp[6]. These feelings can radiate outward to the shoulders and arms and travel the length of your spine. And yes, they're even known to sweep across the chest, genitals, thighs and legs. Not bad for an earful of sound! Even better, it seems that music was the stimulus most frequently reported to create thrills – beating sex, sports, beautiful paintings and sculptures. This experiment postulated that musical thrills might result from spreading electrical activity in the brain, extending through neural links to the limbic and autonomic nervous system[7].

A study in 1997 by Ponn, Silverman & Frederico found that the opiate-blocking drug Naxolene significantly reduced the pleasure that people experienced while listening to music, suggesting that music might actually produce endorphins – pleasure chemicals – in the brain. Part of music's thrill factor lies in its juxtaposition of tension and release. In many classical compositions the pattern of build-up and delivery is structured into sonata form, which states a theme, develops and transforms it, then restates it with climactic twists.

When the need for stimulation is strong and constant, it can be seen as an 'impulse control disorder'. Some psychologists describe the inability to control impulses as 'reward deficiency syndrome' in which brain pathways fail to deliver adequate satisfaction messages. This can be linked to the lack of focused listening, or the fact that the learner is not fully engaged in the task. The result can be sensation-seeking behaviour, cravings, and the need for immediate gratification. This can be seen in the classroom when pupils are not engaged fully with the music and choose some other form of gratification (like messing around). However, once the music hits a nerve they will soon realise that the experience of immersion in the music is as thrilling as anything else they have ever experienced.

One way of giving immediate gratification to your class is by exposing them to music which motivates, stimulates and energises their minds and attitudes to both themselves and learning. A quick fix with the music will help to deter them from seeking out quick fixes from somewhere else!

So, let's begin to look at when and how you can use music to get your learners feeling good about themselves, good about their work, and proud.

What do I need to do?

- Think about where you want to use the music – classroom, assemblies, in the corridor, at the end of registration, or in an achievement assembly?

- Choose songs where the lyrics are pertinent for the occasion e.g. 'You Can Make It If You Try' before a test, 'What have you done today to make yourself feel proud?' at the end of a lesson. 'We Are the Champions' to develop team spirit.

- Familiarise yourself with the suitable pieces of music.

- Lyrics can be extremely powerful in motivating learners, with the right music and the right lyrics.

How to do this in the classroom

Listening Stage 1

- Give clear instructions to the learners of how you want them to listen, and whether or not you want them to join in.

- Play the music loudly so that it fills the room.

- Get them to focus on the lyrics.

- Get the class to face you, and allow them to have a little space to move, if they want to. It's OK to let go and be stimulated by songs, powerful beats and exciting timbres and textures. 'Get ready ... steady ... thrill rides are a coming. Move to the beat ... stamp your feet ... clap your hands ... sing or rap to the words.'

- When the piece is finished, relax. Give yourself and your learners a minute or so before moving on to the next task.

Listening Stage 2

- Note the track – you may choose to use it again if the learner becomes familiar with the fact that it is linked to becoming motivated, stimulated and energised with celebrating achievement. Make a list of suitable tracks for the students to rock the classroom and use in their own learning space, too.

Suggested Musical Extracts to Use for Motivating, Stimulating and Energising

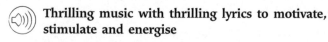 **Thrilling music with thrilling lyrics to motivate, stimulate and energise**

Music with motivational lyrics is the key.

Eddie Murphy – 'I'm a Believer'
Baha Men – 'Best Years of Our lives'
Eddie Cochran – 'C'mon Everybody'
The Proclaimers – 'I'm On My Way'
Heather Small – 'Proud'
Sounds of Blackness – 'You Can Make It If You Try'
Louis Armstrong – 'What a Wonderful World'
Foo Fighters – 'Best of you'
B52s – 'Love Shack'

Queen – 'I Want to Break Free'

Journey – 'Don't Stop Believing'

Nathen Aswell – 'Do That Thing'

Melissa Gordon Rhine – 'Listen to the Sounds of Your Soul'

Success Music – 'Personal Power'

Andrew Loeser – 'Just Believe'

Jan Garrett and J.D. Martin – 'Wonderful World'

The Proclaimers – 'I'm On My Way'

REMEMBER

 *Sound Waves Make Brain Waves* and Make You Feel Proud when you:

- Choose the right extracts with the right lyrics for the occasion.

- Celebrate any type of achievement or give the learners a boost with classroom activities.

- Refer to the Sound Waves Makes Brainwaves by changing the way we feel.

- Fill the room with music at full volume or loud enough to feel the vibrations through your body.

Chapter 4:
More Music With Purpose

Overview

Here are some more suggestions in using music as a learning tool that will boost your ability to utilise this magic box of tricks in your teaching.

Experimental evidence suggests that listening to music enhances people's creativity – an unsurprising discovery, but one whose potential remains largely untapped. Previously in the *Little Book* I have described how you can use music to access different aspects of your mind, alter the state of your autonomic nervous system, and colour your emotional outlook. This chapter brings together all these powers of music to demonstrate how you can use music for timed tasks: Music for Learning to Learn – the X-Factor time zone; taking yourself and your learners to an area where you need to think about confidence and self-belief in Music for Personal Reflection and Realisation; and feeding your brain and body with Musical Snacks.

Feeding the brain with snip-bits of music can help learners move from one task to another or give them a break in their learning. Musical Snacks are the next best thing to chocolate! After all, in today's classrooms, teaching and learning needs to be varied, allowing the students to be motivated and tap into all areas of learning styles and multiple intelligences. Giving them a brain-break with Musical Snacks will allow the transition of learning to go smoothly, preparing the learners for the next activity. We all need snacks occasionally, so use them productively in your classrooms.

Music for Learning to Learn

The X-Factor Time Zone

There has been a great deal of attention paid to Accelerated Learning in classrooms over the last decade. Many teachers are keen to know how using music can raise standards of learning and teaching. Sometimes, considering which music to use, when to use it, and how best to make it effective, often seems a little bit complicated. However, with a bit of forethought, this process can be much simpler.

Here you will discover how quick and easy it is to implement some of these techniques with the aid of the correct musical extracts and their effective application in learning. The X-Factor time task is superb for quick thinking and getting the learners to understand that they have 'X' amount of time to think and complete a task.

Six questions to consider with the X-Factor timed task are:

1. What needs to be done here?
2. Why is this necessary?
3. Where should it be done?
4. When should it be done?
5. How should it be done?
6. Who should do it?

Music can provide the cue you need for each of these questions, and condition your learners to explore particular queries with music. Each extract will link with the key questions by stimulating aspects of the brain specific for that type of task. When you have found something that works, use the same selections for the same questions in subsequent problems. Soon, the learners will be able to prompt the questions themselves by establishing the correct mood for each of these areas of enquiry. Think about the mood or scene you want to create then use the knowledge you have gleaned so far from this *Little Book* to determine the extract. If it is emotional change, then use Relaxation and Calm, if it is Study Skills, then use the Learning and Focus techniques chapter. This *Little Book* will hep you determine the route you want to take with the Learning to Learn extracts. Remember the Beta, Theta, Delta and Alpha Waves I have mentioned so far: music is an invaluable tool in developing thinking skills.

Areas of learning and thinking that suit the X-Factor timed task are:

- Brainstorming, or 'thought showers'.

- Reflective music – supporting individual learning and thinking.

- Spiritual/Meditation – a time for calm and deep thought.

- Music for group tasks (10 Minutes).

- Music for individual tasks (5 minutes).

- Music to support/reflect thinking and learning – evaluation of work.

- Tidy-up Time, or getting back to task/space.

The creative phases can be classed as:

- Preparation – research, study and analysis.

- Incubation of information – subconscious meditation.

- Illumination of learning and thinking – the AHA theory.

- Verification – the implementation of the learning and thinking into practise.

Preparation – research, study and analysis

Firstly, using the music, define the problem, need or desire of learning. Gather information, include big picture and ideas from other fields.

With brainstorming, the idea is to generate a free flow of ideas without initially judging them. The key is to make as many thoughtful connections as you can so that you will generate as many great ideas as possible. This way you generate a 'snowball' effect of creative ideas. It has been found to be more effective if the learners do this on their own first, and then share their ideas in a group[8].

Set up criteria for the best solutions or responses. Tell the students that their ideas need to be imaginative, creative, unique and valuable[9], and then brainstorm solutions.

Choose the musical extracts that make you and your learners feel confident: jazz or musical soundtracks are good. Let the ongoing innovation of sounds inspire you and the learners, and the ideas will start to rain as the music plays. Without judgment, this will shield any learners who are unsure of their own thought droplets.

If the students are working in a group, assign one person to be the scribe. Let the learners' 'rainfall' also inspire other 'thought showers'. Don't let the rain stop until the music fades. Let them freely associate, write, draw or doodle their ideas, using the music as a source of stimulation until the end of the track.

You can also use music as a primer before they brainstorm.

Incubation – subconscious meditation

Step back from the problem for a while in order to allow the subconscious mind time to come up with novel solutions. This is down time, surrendering and letting go, thinking without conscious awareness. Incubation is a Zen-like state of not thinking about the problem, but a chance to have a little music interlude. Incubation listening means focusing on the music and not on the problem. Make available Post-It notes, writing equipment, and so on, but don't force the learners into thinking about what they will later write down. Get them to treat the music as a welcome break from the hard task of problem solving. Repeat this as necessary to trigger the subconscious mind.

Illumination – AHA!

Ideas suddenly arrive, whether whole or in part, to form the basis of the solution. Since this might be an unexpected event, you can't schedule music for these moments. But once the learners have committed their ideas to paper, play your favourite celebration extract as mentioned in the *Motivation* chapter (page 69), as this will make them confident and pleased. This will energise and stimulate them for further insights in future.

Verification – implementation of the idea

Test the results against the criteria established in the first chapter. However, if your problem-solving process extends over weeks, you might want to use a wider range of musical extracts. The music previously heard will make suggested links with completed tasks, and make sure you re-arrange the music to synthesise new formations. When you undertake a new project remember to test, use and implement new musical extracts.

Responses from learners in the past have included:

'The music wakes my natural brilliance and the light bulb starts flashing.'

'Music to me is creative energy.'

'I believe in new and better ideas when I have music to think with.'

'I believe and create multiple solutions when I have music with my brainstorming work.'

'Being energised makes me creative.'

'Music unsticks my mind and I can go anywhere with my ideas.'

'My ideas flow with music.'

'Listening to music is a magical adventure – a journey of thinking and learning.'

'My subconscious delivers the insight I need.'

'My brain doesn't wobble with music – you know when you think it goes la-la sometimes, instead my body wobbles with the beat and I get straight, no nonsense thinking.'

'Each musical idea I hear triggers an image of thought in my mind – I love it.'

'Listening to music is an adventure, I never know how my brain is going to react – but normally it works well for me – my brain that is!'

'I love it (music that is) – it's better than trying to eat chocolate in secret!'

'Musical complexity gives me strength and belief in myself that I can learn and think.'

What do I need to do?

- Decide the type of task. Get your selection of music ready and choose your set time for the task (X-Factor). If the learners are brainstorming or thinking, it is important to choose music without lyrics.

How to do this in the classroom

Listening Stage 1

Explain that *Sound Waves Make Brain Waves* by playing different types of music linked with the X-Factor and that the rush of a timed task will increase the adrenaline and pump up the heart rate, so that a sense of urgency and excitement occurs.

- Set the task. The key is to have clear learning expectations. Tell them how you want them to listen and engage in the task, and whether or not you want them to jot down notes. The more direction you give them, the better the understanding.

- Give the learners the X-Factor Time (how long the piece of music will be played for and the length of the task).

- Play the music at a medium level so that the thinking process is not fully interrupted.

- Once the music has started (30 seconds or so) you can turn the volume up a little so it fills the room.

- When the piece is finished, thrill in the buzz of energy in the room.

Listening Stage 2

- In some cases you might like to play the music for a second time, letting the learners develop their initial responses to the task. Make a note of the track – you may choose to use this track again if the learners become familiar with the fact that it is linked to X-Factor learning, which are timed tasks.

• Offer the name of the musical extract and where the learner could get it for free; they could use it for homework.

The correct Sound Waves will make and create the correct Brain Waves! In this way, pupils will be able to effectively use music themselves in their own learning.

Suggested Musical Extracts to Use for Learning to Learn

Timed Task Extracts that can suit all types of Accelerated Learning Techniques, Thinking Skills and Self-Evaluation. Extracts range from 90–165 BPM depending on the nature of the task in hand

Learning to Learn

Brainstorming (1-6 minute excerpts)

'Captain Scarlet's Theme' – Classic 1960s TV themes (fast) 2 mins

'Dream Chunnate'– Takyal folk song (fast) 4 mins

'Cu Chullain' – Adiemus Live – (fast) 6 mins

'21 Seconds' – Ambulance – (fast) 3 mins

Reflective – Individual Learning (15 minutes slow mix)

'Time to Say Goodbye' – The Magic Orchestra

'Aquarium'– Relaxing Classics

'Facades' – The Classics: Minimalist

Spiritual/Meditation - (5 minutes)

'An Ending' - Very Best of Chillout Gold

Group Task - 10 Minutes

'Arachnaphobia' - The Big Screen Collection
'Hook' - Music from the Spielberg Film
'Jurassic Park' - Music from the Spielberg Film
'Raiders of the Lost Ark'- Music from the Spielberg Film

Individual Task - 10 Minutes

'Breaking of the Fellowship' - Music from *Lord of the Rings*
'May it be' - Enya

Meditation/Supportive

'Capriccio for Chinese Flute' - Takyal folk music
'Soukka Stars' - Takyal folk music
'A Takyal Folk Song' - Takyal folk music

REMEMBER

 *Sound Waves Make Brain Waves* with the X-Factor when you:

Use extracts with 90–165 BPM.

- Make sure your timed-task extracts have no lyrics (if you are expecting a written response).

- Clearly indicate the length of time learners have to complete the task.

- Adjust the volume level at medium to high.

- Develop your collection of extracts by looking at timed advert slots that fit your activities, for example, the *Countdown* theme, or the theme to *Mission Impossible*.

Music for Personal Reflection and Realisation

Music for Me

We live in a world which is fast, furious and often frantic. We have a tendency to forget about ourselves as individuals and instead spend a great deal of time working to satisfy others. Learners also work hard to satisfy their teachers and families and often do not have the time to talk about or reflect upon their successes and triumphs.

'Jamming for joy' is as old as music itself, and it's widely agreed that music operates at psychological, emotional, aesthetic, social, cultural and spiritual levels to help us have fun and uplift our bodies and minds. But its mood-busting powers can also be used in a more specific and useful way than that. The elevating music we can use stimulates optimism, breaks emotional paralysis and provides us all – teachers and learners – with a natural energy lift. Think of it as an antidepressant with no side effects.

The music suggested in this chapter can help you and your learners with temporary sadness, setbacks and depression, negative or recurrent thoughts, shyness, confidence and inner belief. When suffering with disappointment, failure or loss, feeling paralysed, hopeless or fatigued, music can induce elated mood, raise psychological arousal, providing an easy way to be proactive.

For learners who experience unwanted or intrusive thoughts, obsessing over a problem or detail, music creates a positive outlook to clear negative ideas from the mind, and acts as a distraction. Anxious learners who find it difficult to interact with people effectively, and have limited self-belief, are all too apparent in today's classrooms. Lift their spirits and energy by using music. Create a shared feeling and stimulate their systems to alleviate fear of rejection.

When you think of mood, words such as 'happiness' and 'sadness' might come to mind and we speak of 'elated', 'depressed' and 'neutral' moods. No matter how you choose to term it, the latest research into biochemistry and mood indicates that where you sit on the happy-to-sad spectrum can affect how you and your students work, relate, eat, sleep and feel about themselves. Many learners just wish to feel better about themselves.

One of the best ways to boost your mood musically is to do it gradually – starting at a slow or moderate pace, close to the way you or the pupils are feeling, and getting more uplifted with each selection. Learners who listen in this way report feeling relaxed but excited, with increased energy and spirit. Take advantage of this mood induction to create your own graduated CD.

Start with slow or mid-tempo music that matches the way the learners tend to feel when they are shy or lacking in confidence. Make each selection gradually faster, more upbeat, and higher in pitch. Be careful, though – pushing the mood change too fast can make your learners anxious and resentful. Limit the listening time to what you feel will be reasonable for the class at that time. After musical mood induction, people are able to remove selected intrusive thoughts and are less threatened by stimuli that might trigger phobic reactions. Using music for these types of learners can help them escape certain types of phobia, like worrying about writing and spelling incorrectly, or talking in front of the class. You will be amazed at the amount of learners in our classrooms today who have 'phobic' type tendencies when exposed to aspects of learning they are not confident with.

Music for personal reflection and realisation was originally prepared for groups of learners who were disaffected with school and life, lacked confidence and had no personal aspirations. One solution is to realise that we are all 'special' in our own way, that we have many wonderful qualities as individuals and we need to celebrate these qualities and to take time to feel good about what we do in life.

This category of music is also intended to help all ages to feel good about themselves. It will help individuals take time to reflect on the successes of the day. Music is a wonderful tool for building confidence in your learners, especially if they are living lives which swing wildly between turbulent and smooth, disjointed and calm.

Use each extract in the suggested list to help your students reflect upon the successes of the day – in work, relationships or family – and take time to focus upon what they have learned from their experiences.

Use music to improve your mood and raise psychological arousal, preparing the way to be positive and proactive in everything you want to do. Music can boost morale, enthusiasm and motivation, so that much more can be achieved. Music can erase negative or unwanted thoughts and it can take you to a place of harmony and inner beauty. These extracts will create a positive outlook to clear the negative thoughts from your mind and will act as a distraction for you and your pupils. Visualisation through music is the technique to boost music's mood-lifting power. Think of it as a golden light, filling your mind, and let each beat that you hear make the light brighter. Music can help you and your learners feel happier – so use music for a quick lift when you need one.

What do I need to do?

- Know your students – especially if they are susceptible to erratic mood changes. If they are, and you are both anxious about it, music will help them control the mood swings.

- Decide if you are going to present the musical extract to an individual or to the whole class. It is important to choose music that fits the occasion. Mood induction – using music to help people access a particular state – is key to helping all learners become more focused and happy with themselves.

How to do this in the classroom

Listening Stage 1

- This type of music will transform you and your learners to approach tasks and activities in your classroom. They will enjoy and appreciate the elevated states they will experience.

- Set clear instructions for the learners – how you want them to listen and engage. Begin by explaining how they are to sit and listen and that it's fine to let go and be stimulated by the music. Powerful beats or soothing textures and timbres can all be effective in the right environment.

- Play the music at medium volume level so that the mood changing process is not fully interrupted. If the volume is changed drastically for no given reason then you will spark a break in the way they are focusing on the music.

- Allow the students to express themselves however they wish.

- Watch, listen and see the learners responding.

- When the piece is finished, tell the learners to soak up the emotional change in their bodies and minds. Let them have some quiet time to be fully immersed in the emotional experience of the music. Think of this as being like a sponge soaking up water.

Listening Stage 2

- Keep a note of the track – you may choose to use this track again as the learners become familiar with the fact that it is a mood inductive tool.

- Offer the name of the musical extract and where the learner could get it for free; you'll be surprised at the amount of requests you will get.

Suggested Musical Extracts to Use for Personal Reflection and Realisation

Music for Me – Mood Induction

Personal Reflection and Realisation

These tracks are a combination of relaxation and motivational music.

BPM range from 80–165 BPM. Select them specifically for your needs.

Reflection

1. 'Schindler's List'
2. 'Like Jesus to a Child'
3. 'Intermezzo'
4. 'Molly'
5. 'Largo'
6. 'Up Where We belong'
7. 'Feather Fly'
8. 'Empire of the Sun'
9. 'Colour Purple'
10. 'Where Dreams Are Born'

Realisation – Music to Enthuse and Create Personal Potential

11. 'Bad Reputation'
12. 'Hallelujah'
13. 'Duelling Banjos'
14. 'Flop Eared Mule'
15. 'Clinch Mountain Backstop'
16. 'City Madness'
17. 'Back to the Future'
18. 'Mad Max'
19. 'Sudden Impact'

REMEMBER

 *Sound Waves Make Brain Waves* with Music for Me when you:

- Use music for confidence and emotional well-being.

- Choose music that will affect how you and your learners will respond to the way you work and feel about yourselves.

- Try out different pieces of music to find the appropriate balance for the right occasion.

- Use extracts with a NPM range from 80–165 BPM.

- Be kind to your heart, mind and body.

Music for Learning and Focus

Musical Snacks

Music is a great way of creating learning links in your lessons. These help pupils change from one task to another whilst at the same time helping to prepare and energise the brain and mind for the next stage in learning.

So, in order to break up activities or tasks in your lessons, give the class a musical snack – music to energise the brain. A one-minute excerpt will prepare them for the next task or activity and also give you time to reflect and evaluate your work and theirs. If you wish, call it a Brain Break; it's a brief pause to give you the time to reflect and prepare the learner for the next part of the lesson.

These extracts can be used in any way you feel will support your pupils to become more stimulated, motivated and energised in their learning and in the development of their thought processes during lessons. You may also choose to calm the pupils as they move from an energised, focused task to a more reflective moment in learning. As the teacher and provider of learning stimulus, you will be able to judge how you need to change the environmental make-up of your classroom or learning space.

What do I need to do?

- Explain to the learners what a Musical Snack is – food for the brain. A musical snack is a break in learning where you feed the brain with music like you feed the body with food.

- Decide the purpose of the Musical Snack: it might just be a break from one activity to another, or a quick way of altering the emotional state of the class. If you need to energise, use the Energy Snack Tracks, if you need to calm and get them focused, use the Calm Track Snacks, and if you just need to get them moving from one group or area in the classroom to another use the Moving-Grooving Snack Tracks

How to do this in the classroom

Listening Stage 1

- These Sound Waves make the right Brain Waves because they are different and fit each purpose depending on their focus. Try a snack or two and see … the proof is in the pudding!

- Provide clear instructions explaining how you want the students to *listen* or *move* or just have *quiet reflection time*. One minute can seem a lifetime when listening effectively to the music.

- Explain clearly that it's Musical Snack Time and what you want them to do: listen, energise, or move or groove. Play the music and take time for yourself as well as focusing on the learners in order to prepare for the next stage. The Musical Snacks are breaks in the learning and lesson. You'll be amazed how effective one minute of music can be.

Listening Stage 2

- Finish playing the musical track and then use the key words 'Focus for Learning'. I have used this key phrase frequently with my students so that they know they are going to be involved in an activity. You will see that giving the class a one-minute Musical Snack will get them ready for the next stage.

- Make sure you note the date, time and task presented with this extract, as you do not want to play the same one all the time: variety is the spice of life. Or, if you wish to choose set tracks for set types of Brain Breaks, then this could get the learners in a routine for knowing the type of Brain Break you are giving them simply by hearing the musical snack you are playing. Remember that the Brain and Mind needs to be energised frequently during a lesson.

Suggested Musical Extracts to Use for Musical Snacks

Musical Snack Tracks

All of these tracks have been chosen for the musical timbres and textures, and fit each occasion because of the wide range of beats per minute. These vary from 80–160 BPM.

The Beach Boys – 'Good Vibrations'
Katrina and the Waves – 'Walking on Sunshine'
The Pointer Sisters – 'Yes, We Can Can'
Pratt/McClain – Theme from 'Happy Days'
Jerry Lee Lewis – 'Great Balls of Fire'
Spencer Davies Group – 'Gimme Some Lovin'
Kylie Minogue – 'Locomotion'
Van Halen – 'Jump'
Stealers Wheelers – 'Stuck in the Middle with You'
Jackatta – 'American Dream'
Wang Chung – 'Everybody Have Fun Tonight'
Blue Suede – 'Hooked on a Feeling'
Danny and the Juniors – 'At the Hop'
Chubby Checker – 'Let's Twist Again'
Eddie Cochran – 'C'mon Everybody'
Bobby McFerrin – 'Don't Worry, Be Happy'
Paul Simon – 'Have a Good Time'
Gerry and the Pacemakers – 'I Like It'
Dobie Gray – 'The In Crowd'
EMF – 'Unbelievable'
Duran Duran – 'Electric Barbarella'

Musical Snack Tracks – Calm Snack Tracks

Libera – 'Salva Me'
Karl Jenkins – 'Dawn Dancing'
Karl Jenkins – 'The Wooing of Etain'
Brian Eno – 'Music for Airports'
Michael Jones – 'Pianoscapes'
Erik Satie – 'Gymnopedies'

Lanz and Speer – 'Desert Vision'

J.S. Bach – 'Air on a G String'

Randy Crafton – 'Inner Rhythms'

Liz Story – 'Solid Colours'

Ennio Morricone – Soundtrack from *The Mission*: 'On Earth as It Is in Heaven'

Hans Zimmer – Soundtrack from *Gladiator*: 'Now We Are Free'

Geoffrey Burgon – Soundtrack from *Brideshead Revisited*: 'Orphans of the Storm'

Michael Nyman – Soundtrack from *The Piano*: 'The Heart Asks Pleasure'

Barber – 'Adagio for Strings'

Earl Klugh – 'Late Night Guitar'

Peter White – 'Confidential'

Mooving–Grooving Snack Tracks

Eddie Murphy – Soundtrack from *Shrek*: 'I'm a Believer'

Arrow – 'Hot, Hot, Hot'

Devo – 'Whip It'

The Turtles – 'Happy Together'

Ray Charles – 'Let the Good Times Roll'

Mary J. Blige – 'Be Happy'

MC Hammer – 'U Can't Touch This'

The Cars – 'Shake It Up'

Jerry Lee Lewis – 'Great Balls of Fire'

Ritchie Valens – 'La Bamba'

Reel 2 Reel – 'I Like to Move It'

Michael Buffer – 'Let's Get Ready to Rumble'

BTO - 'You Ain't Seen Nothing Yet'
Bad Manners - 'Can Can'
Adam Ant - 'Goody Two Shoes'
The Pointer Sisters - 'I'm So Excited'
Van Halen - 'Jump'
Real McCoy - 'Another Night'
The Quad City DJs (The Train) - 'C'Mon 'n Ride It'
Argent - 'Hold your Head Up'

REMEMBER

 *Sound Waves Make Brain Waves* with Musical Snacks when you:

- Break up the lesson and move between one activity to another with a quick Brain Break.

- Play each extract for only a minute or so to provide a break and to feed the mind with energy and stimulation.

- Choose the right music for the right reason and use extracts with BPM between 80 and 165.

- Build your own library of short extracts as your confidence in applying music to your lessons grows.

Chapter 5:
And Finally

Overview

The journey you have taken in this *Little Book of Music* has brought us to the final chapter where we wrap it all up and take it all away, experimenting with what has been written, tried and tested, and discovered by you up to this point.

This book has directed you to a specific way of using music as a learning tool, or method of changing behaviour, emotional make-up and celebration. But wait, beware, there are some aspects of using music that could be detrimental to you and your learners if music is used in an inappropriate way.

Some of you will argue that this chapter should be at the beginning, but you are wrong! Without trying and testing the theories and applications, you would not have known how powerful music can be for learning. Yes, silence can be golden and if you play the wrong music at the wrong time then you are not creating the right Sound Waves for the right Brain Waves.

No doubt your musical learning journey with this *Little Book of Music* has given you food for thought, and it has been tried and tested by hundreds of teachers and thousands of learners. By now, you will have added your name to the list too – that is, if you have given it a go.

Let me end with where the music begins. Remember the material from Memory Recall? Have you tried it? If you had played music whilst reading this book, your Memory Recall of all the wonderful uses of music that's in here would now be easier and more accessible for you to apply in your classrooms. So, if you haven't tried it with this book, then next time you need to remember something, do as the *Little Book* says ... the right music at the right time for the right reasons will support *Sound Waves Make Brain Waves*.

Caution! The Right Music at the Right Time for the Right Reasons

Choosing the Right Music

When choosing the right music it is essential that you consider many factors. At this stage, you should now have a good idea of implementing music effectively in your learning environment. Your confidence as a teacher should have grown but you *must* make sure your choices fit the right criteria for using music as a learning tool. Remember: the right type of music for the right type of reasons. You may not find the perfect music every time but experience and application is the key.

Here are five important questions to consider when it comes to making the right choices:

1. What type of emotional state do you want to create?
2. What is the right volume for the occasion?
3. Have you got music with the right instrumentation?
4. Do you need a piece with soloist, jazz group, choir, electronic music, orchestral, songs, rock or pop music?
5. Consider the age range of your learners and bear in mind the generation gap. Music that might appeal to you might not always appeal to them.

Much of the music suggested in this book fits a specific learning process: it's not about using *any* type of music. This is an essential consideration when choosing music for your lessons. And take into account the cultural influences, background and heritage of all your students.

Beware of working to the 'wrong' music! Do not let yourself or the learners fall into the trap of using any type of music which, in the long run, could have an adverse effect on what you are trying to create in your learning environment. Follow the suggestions in this book for music that stimulates your mind. Feel your neurons fire up as the first sweet strains of musically generated electrical energy flow through your cortex.

Remember, you can also use your musical repertoire for other mental tasks and activities in your life:

- Add a soundtrack to your social preparations by blasting uplifting selections while you get dressed for an occasion. Think of it as dressing up your mind.

- Socialise your ears with speakers rather than headphones, to get accustomed to the environment of shared sound waves in the air.

- Take your show on the road. Listen to uplifting music in the car on the way to work or a special event, so you arrive full of life and confidence.

- Associate these sounds with your mind's finest moments, and all the natural neurological benefits of music will be yours. Remember, *Sound Waves Make Brain Waves*.

Silence Can Be Golden Too!

No Music

Music is great, otherwise I would not have written this little book, but I also have to offer you a very big warning:

Silence really can be golden.

If used to extremes, musical saturation can occur and the negative effects can start to out-weigh the benefits. The music will lose its potency and your learners may become agitated as well as disaffected.

Utilise music selectively and purposefully at all times. Think of the 10–30 rule. Only play music between 10 and 30 per cent of the total learning time in your lesson, with the following exceptions, of course:

1. When music forms part of the curriculum.
2. When teaching languages and you need to be singing to develop vocabulary.
3. When used in assemblies or celebration opportunities, supporting the emotional context of the occasion.

REMEMBER:

Too much music is as bad as none at all.

When studying music, good teachers tell learners that the musical rests are as important as the written notes on paper. The moments of silence define the musical sounds. This is the same as music in your every day life. Magical Moments of Silence – or as I tell my learners, Quiet Time – is a great time for reflection, too. These times shape and strengthen the sounds that surround you.

Natural pauses in the listening process give time for your brain to re-charge. Sometimes I need to turn off the music in my car so that I can listen to my own thoughts, because my mind is being saturated with too many musical sounds and I'm not reaping the benefits and rewards. Not to mention the fact that there's a lot of 'dodgy' music (as the learners say) on the radio, too! Quiet, while not the same as silence, is still an acceptable balance to music, speech and noise. Silence gives meaning to the sound and works to maximise music's amazing impact on your life. Remember, even though you might not have music playing, there will still be invisible sound waves in the air. So, in a different sense, invisible sound waves also make great brain waves.

This Is Where the End Begins!

Getting Started

You need to get started with:

- The right equipment
- The right music
- The right frame of mind

Throughout this book you have learnt about the philosophy, research and correct application of using Music and the Mind through *Sound Waves Make Brain Waves*. Here is where the fun begins!

Much of what you are about to embark on will be linked with your inner belief, as a real teacher in a real classroom, that music *can* and *will* make a difference to you and your students. This book is about truth and honesty and making it work. If it doesn't work first time – don't give up. Believe in yourself, believe in the power of the music you have at hand and be strong in your willingness and eagerness to break the rules and be different.

When training teachers and other educationalists, I often have hundreds of music tracks with me, but of course I can't play them all at once. It's about knowing your audience, testing the water, and applying the techniques in this book to improve standards of learning and teaching.

So good luck, with the following tips: try, try, try, fall and pick yourself up again, enjoy, be happy, and learn from the overriding philosophy behind Music and the Mind – that *Sound Waves Make Brain Waves*.

The Right Equipment

- CD Player
- Music Tracks
- Computer
- MP3 Player
- IPod
- Hi-Fi
- Radio

The Right Music

- Choose your tracks carefully
- Start small – grow with confidence
- Try using your own music, too
- Refer to the book – keep checking – right music for right occasion

The Right Frame of Mind

- Be confident
- Try, try, again
- Get motivated

- Forgive yourself when it goes wrong

- Celebrate when it goes right

- Take charge of yourself and your learners

- Enjoy

- Be happy

- Love the music and love yourself for the great job that you do as a teacher

- Tell yourself: 'I'm great'

- Tell your learners: 'You're great'

- Believe in *Sound Waves Make Brain Waves*

AND REMEMBER:

Music expresses that which cannot be said and on which it is impossible to be silent.

– Victor Hugo

Appendices

Appendix A: Top Tips for Getting Music Cheap as Chips or Fantastically FREE!

In the current climate, with easy access to the internet there are many ways of getting music free (or at least very cheaply). Here are some of my best tips (including websites) where you can get great music for free, or you can play it 'live' in your classroom.

1. Sounds obvious, but ask friends or colleagues if they have any used or old music (records, tapes or CDs) they no longer want. Listen to your heart's content – their rubbish is your gold dust!

2. Car boot sales, jumble sales or school fairs.

3. Stores that buy or exchange music.

4. Public Library – they loan music for free!

5. Bargain buckets in your supermarket or local petrol station.

6. Download music free off the internet.

7. Sponsorship from your local store or businesses where you can offer them promotional space in your

school newsletter or magazine. (I got some blank CDs from a local shop and gave them a mix of tracks to play in their own shop.)

8. Grants from Teaching Councils such as the GTCW or GTC. You could carry out small-scale action research studies and build a portfolio of music from CDs, iTunes and other sources, so that you are able to have an impact on learning and teaching in your own classrooms. I did, so you can!

9. Exchange CDs with friends or colleagues.

10. Your learners – let them bring in music from various (legal!) sources.

11. Compile your own music: you and/or the learners create your own CDs or music catalogues.

12. Most excitingly: learner compositions. A thrilling moment in any learner's life is when you put a piece of their work on display in the classroom. Many of our young musicians these days compose some truly original pieces of work which should, could and need to be celebrated and shared with others. One example is a GCSE music student who composed a piece of film music that was emotionally astounding. Another example is the A-level music student who composed a song to celebrate Fairtrade Week which was played in the school and at local supermarkets to celebrate the links between the school, local supermarket and Fairtrade distributors. A Key Stage 3 learner composed an ostinato piece (the use of repeated rhythmic and melodic patterns) using ICT with synthesised sounds – the musical layering, timbres

and textures were superb. So, you don't always have to *buy* music. You can use the music created by your own students, and they will be pleased as punch that their work is being shared and experienced by others.

Great websites for great music

www.hypergurl.com/musicsounds.html

www.radioblogclub.com

www.deezer.com

www.freeplaymusic.com

www.listen.com

www.napster.com

www.musicnow.com

www.findanymusic.com

www.my-free-music.com/home.htm

www.bresso.com

www.limewire.com

www.hearmusic.com

www.anymusicdownloads.com

www.mrband.com

www.youtube.com

www.peaceloveproductions.com/freemusic.html

www.premiumbeat.com/music-for-website/

www.music.podshow.com/

www.royaltyfreemusic.com/loops-for-powerpoint-flash-web.html

www.abc.net.au/triplej/listen/mp3s.htm

www.marcgunn.com/articles/celtic-music-downloads.shtml

A Word of Caution

Make sure when you are downloading any music that you have permission to do so. Many of us would rather pay a few pence for authentic recordings than cause waves with illegal downloads. You are the person who has to take responsibility for what you choose to access and download on the internet. If it is freely available, then you are able to use it in your work. However, be careful with some sites that have made slight alterations to original recordings if they do not have copyright permission of the original artist.

All schools should have a licence to play musical recordings for educational purposes, and if you are not sure, then ask your headteacher or local authority if this is the case.

As teachers, we can now use ICT to support and help us in every way, and using music correctly will indeed make your teaching and the learning in your classrooms truly spectacular.

So, seek and ye shall find music for free – if you want it badly enough. Good luck with your treasure hunt.

Appendix B: The Best Nine Compilation CD Music Box Set for Learning in the World ... Ever!

Apart from the musical extracts suggested earlier in this Little Book, here is a wealth of music tracks which I use all the time. Try them and remember: *Sound Waves Make Brain Waves*.

Great Up-Beat 'Dance' Music

Wham – 'Wake Me Up Before You Go Go'
Dead or Alive – 'You Spin Me Round'
Men at Work – 'Down Under'
Cyndi Lauper – 'She Bop'
The Police – 'Every Little Thing She Does Is Magic'
The Pretenders – 'Don't Get Me Wrong'
Katrina and the Waves – 'Walking on Sunshine'
The Bangles – 'Walk Like an Egyptian'
Madness – 'Our House'
Michael Jackson – 'Don't Stop 'Til You Get Enough'
Joe Jackson – 'You Can't Get What You Want'
ABC – 'Be Near Me'
The Go-Gos – 'Vacation'
Joe Jackson – 'Stepping Out'
The Hues Corporation – 'Rock the Boat'
Heatwave – 'Boogie Nights'
ABBA – 'Dancing Queen'
Chic – 'Dance, Dance, Dance

Thelma Houston – 'Don't Leave Me This Way'
KC and The Sunshine Band – 'Shake Your Booty'
The Village People – 'Macho Man'
The Sylvers – 'Boogie Fever'
The Tramps – 'Disco Inferno'
Bee Gees – 'YMCA'

Great Songs for PSHE – Relationships and Working Together

Harry Connick Jr – 'I've Got a Great Idea'
Roberta Flack – 'You Make Me Feel Brand New'
Bobby Darin – 'Fly Me to the Moon'
Eric Clapton – 'Wonderful Tonight'
Ben E. King – 'Stand By Me'
Mary Wells – 'My Guy'
Andy Williams – 'Moon River'
Etta James – 'At Last'
Minnie Riperton – 'Loving You'
Rod Stewart – 'You're in My heart'
Daniel Kobialka – 'Oh What a Beautiful Morning'
Sophie B Hawkins – 'As I Lay Me Down'
Minnie Riperton – 'Loving You'
Lanz and Speer – 'Natural States'
Liz Story – 'Solid Colours'
Michael Hedges – 'Aerial Boundaries'
Righteous Brothers – 'You're My Soul and Inspiration'
Eddie Rabbit & Crystal Gayle – 'You and I'

Move with Motown for Energy and Soothe with Jazz for Calm

Motown

Jackie Wilson – 'Higher and Higher'
Dionne Warwick – 'Walk on By'
Diana Ross and The Supremes – 'Baby Love'
Gladys Night and The Pips – 'Midnight Train to Georgia'
Stevie Wonder – 'Superstition'
The Four Tops – 'I Can't Help Myself'
Sam & Dave – 'Soul Man'
Fontella Bass – 'Rescue Me'
The Temptations – 'My Girl'

Soothing Jazz

Spyro Gyra – 'Collection'
Jim Hall – 'Emily'
Tom Scott – 'Night Creatures'
Earl Klugh – 'Late Night Guitar'
Dan Siegel – 'Northern Nights'
The Rippingtons – Tourist in Paradise'
Richard Elliott – 'Ricochet'
Peter White – 'Confidential'

Brilliant School Songs

The Ramones – 'Rock 'n' Roll High School
The Sylvers – 'High School Dance'
Herman's Hermits – 'Don't Know Much About History'

Gary US Bonds – 'School Is In'
Lou Reed – 'Teach the Gifted Children'
Chuck Berry – 'School Days'
Klaatu – 'A Million Miles Away'
Beach Boys – 'All Dressed Up for School'
Pink Floyd – 'Another Brick in the Wall'
Deftones – 'Back to School'
The Four Tops – 'Back to School Again'
Madness – 'Baggy Trousers'
Twisted Sister – 'Be Chrool to Your Scuel'
Eminem – 'Brain Damage'
The Beatles – 'Getting Better'
Otis Rush – 'Homework'
The Clash – 'Mark Me Absent'
Atom and His Package – 'Punk Rock Academy'

Music to End a Lesson – Leaving Songs

Peter, Paul & Mary – 'Leaving on a Jet Plane'
Dale Evans – 'Happy Trails'
Wyonna – 'Is It Over Yet?'
Jim Reeves – 'Adios, Amigos'
Ray Charles – 'Hit the Road, Jack'
Sarah Brightman & Andrea Bocelli – 'Time to Say Goodbye'
Semisonic – 'Closing Time'
Louis Armstrong – 'What a Wonderful World'
The Vogues – 'Five O' Clock World'
OMD – 'If You Leave'

Sonny & Cher – 'Baby Don't Go'
Green Day – 'Good Riddance'
Elton John – 'Goodbye Yellow Brick Road'
Michael Johnson – 'Bluer than Blue'
Rascal Flatts – 'I'm Movin On'
Jim Croce – 'Time in a Bottle'
Eric Clapton – 'Tears in Heaven'
Leanne Rimes – 'Leaving's Not Leavin'
Bette Midler – 'Wind Beneath My Wings'
The Little River Band – 'Cool Change'

'Groovy' Songs to Make Your Heart Sing

Paul McCartney/ Wings – 'Roll It'
Beatles – 'Oh Darlin'
Queen – 'We Will Rock You'
Queen – 'We Are the Champions'
Debbie Boone – 'You Light Up My Life'
Berlin – 'Take My Breath Away'
Gloria Gaynor – 'I Will Survive'
Jimmy Cliff – 'Don't Worry Be Happy'
Tosh and Jagger – 'Don't Look Back in Anger'
Tracy Chapman – Give Me One Good Reason'
Marc Hunter – 'I'm in the Spotlight'
0155 – 'Looking for an Echo'
John Farnam – 'Paradise'
Baha Men – 'Who Let the Dogs Out'
Chris James – 'We Are Angels'
Jimmy Cliff – 'Wonderful World, Beautiful People'

Joe Cocker & Jennifer Warne – 'Up Where We Belong'
Cyndi Lauper – 'Girls Just Want to Have Fun'
Pretenders – 'Brass in Pocket'
Rolling Stones – 'Emotional Rescue'
Bruce Springsteen – 'Dancing in the Dark'
Bruce Springsteen – 'Born in the USA'
Tina Turner – 'Simply the Best'
Bob Dylan – 'Like a Rolling Stone'
Aretha Franklin – 'Respect'
The Beatles – 'Let It Be'

Interactive Learner Songs – Pair Share Return

Sharing with your learner

Run DMC – 'You Talk Too Much'
The Chiffons – 'Sweet Talkin' Guy'
Rufus – 'Tell Me Something Good'
Harry Nilsson – 'Tell It Like it is'
The Coasters – 'Yakety Yak'
Jackson 5 – 'ABC'
Marv Johnson – 'You Got What It Takes'

Back to work on your own!

The Beatles – 'Get Back'
Elvis Presley – 'Easy Come Easy Go'
Maxine Nightingale – 'Right Back Where We Started'
Jackson 5 – 'Never Can Say Goodbye'
Simon & Garfunkel – 'Homeward Bound'
Peaches & Herb – 'Reunited'
KC & The Sunshine Band – 'That's the Way I Like It'

Classical Music Tracks to Die for!

Baroque Music

Vivaldi – 'Four Seasons'
J.S. Bach – 'Brandenburg Concertos'
G.F. Handel – 'Water Music'
A.Corelli – 'Concerti Grosso'

Classical Music

Haydn – 'Symphony No. 48 in C'
Beethoven – '5th Symphony Opus 67 in C Minor'
Mendelssohn – 'Violin Concerto in E Minor Opus 64'
Rossini – 'William Tell Overture'

Romantic Music

Debussy – 'Bergamasque'
Brahms – 'German Requiem'
Verdi – 'La Traviata'
Dvorak – 'Symphony No. 9 in E Minor'

20th Century Music

Holst – 'Planets Suite'
Bartok – 'Hungarian Folk Songs'
Mahler – 'Symphony No. 8'
Stravinsky – 'The Rite of Spring'

Songs that you can't stop singing – for the healthy and happy learners

Little Eva – 'Locomotion'
Bill Hayley and the Comets – 'Rock Around the Clock'
Jerry Lee Lewis – 'Great Balls of Fire'
Bobby Darin – 'Splish Splash'
U2 – 'Beautiful Day'
Beach Boys – 'Kokomo'
The Young Rascals – 'Groovin'
Fleetwood Mac – 'Don't Stop'
Irene Kara – 'What a Feelin'
Kool and the Gang – 'Celebration'
Bill Withers – 'Lovely Day'
The Monkees – 'I'm a Believer'
B52s – 'Love Shack'
Aqua – 'Best Friend'
Mamas & Papas – 'California Dreamin'
James Brown – 'Living in America'
Dennis Brown – 'Money In My pocket'
Kenny Loggins – 'This Is It'
Sheryl Crow – 'Soak Up the Sun'
Wang Chung – 'Everybody Have Fun Tonight'

Appendix C: Using 'Suggestopedia' and 'Jeopardy' for Study and Revision Skills

Often, a learner tries too hard to internalise as much information as possible, for example when they fail to use the correct techniques to simplify the key points and end up highlighting almost everything on the page!

Suggestopedia

An idea from Suggestopedia has worked for many of my own learners. They write key bullet points to the left of the main text or information, and insert a little visual prompt on the right to link the bullet point and main text together. At the end of the study period, instead of looking at the main body of text they focus on the key word/ bullet point and visual cue or diagram to the right. The centre text becomes almost invisible to the eye.

Jeopardy

Another way of simplifying study and revision is to play a version of the 'Jeopardy' game with your own learning. Much like the quiz game, the technique itself is simple. When you arrive at an important passage of information write a question in the margin so that the answer to the question is then in that piece of information. Previous studies have shown that when this is done, learners are faced with the same types of questions in the exam, hence LINKED LEARNING – eureka! See the following websites to help you:

http://www.sonypictures.com/tv/shows/jeopardy/indexflash.php

http://www.hardin.k12.ky.us/res_techn/countyjeopardygames.htm

http://www.techteachers.com/jeopardytemplates.htm

http://www.games.com/game/jeopardy/

http://www.shambles.net/pages/learning/games/jeopardy/

Appendix D: BPM (Beats Per Minute)

Beats Per Minute (BPM) is a unit typically used as either a measure of tempo in music, or a measure of one's heart rate. A rate of 60 bpm means that one beat will occur every second. If you clap or tap in time with the beat this gives you the count per minute. Try it and see.

Contact

Nina Jackson

Do let me know your thoughts on this *Little Book of Music for the Classroom* and any extracts you want me to try too.

You can contact me through Independent Thinking Ltd at:

- www.independentthinking.co.uk

Or e-mail me direct at:

- nina.jackson@independentthinking.co.uk

I look forward to hearing from you – and enjoy your music, whether it be for learning, for yourself or for pleasure.

References

Chapter 1

Alberic, G. (1994). *En Chanson: Pourquoi et Comment, Francais dans le monde*, Paris.

Beentjes, J.W.J., Cees, M.K., & van der Voort, T.H.A. (1996). 'Combining background media with doing homework: Incidence of background media use and perceived effects', *Communication Education ,Volume 45, 59-72.*

Campbell, Don. G. (1997). *The Mozart Effect,* London: Hodder & Stoughton.

Campbell, Don. G. (1983). *Introduction to the Musical Brain,* 2nd Edition, Missouri, MMB

Etaugh, C., & Ptasnik, P. (1982). *Effects of studying to music and post study relaxation on reading comprehension,* Nova University, USA.

Gardner, H. (1997). *The Musical Mind,* – University of Irvine. Califorinia.

Gardner, H. (1983). *Frames of Mind,* Basic Books, USA.

[1]Gilbert, I. (2006). *The Big Book of Independent Thinking,* Crown House Publications, Carmarthen.

Hall, J. (1952). 'The effect of background music on reading comprehension of 278 eighth and ninth graders.' *Journal of Educational Research, Volume 45, 451- 458, USA.*

Hardy, G.H. (1940), *A Mathematician's Apology,* Cambridge: Cambridge Univeristy Press, 1940, p.26

Jourdan, R. (1997). *Music, the brain & ecstasy,* Trade Paperbacks: USA.

Koppelman, D., & Imig, S. (1995). *The Effect of Music on Children's Writing Content,* University of Virginia, Charlottesville, VA. (ERIC Document Reproduction Service No. ED 383 002).

List, G. (1972). *Speech, Melody and Song Melody in Central Thailand,* Intonation, Baltimore: Penguin Books.

Lozanov, G, (c1978). *Suggestology and outlines of Suggestopedy,* translated by Marjorie Hall-Pozharlleva and Krassimira Pashmokova, Gordon & Breach Publications, New York

Nisbet, J. & Watt, J. (1984). Case Study. In J. Bell, T. Bush, A.Fox, J. Goodey and S.Goulding (eds), *Conducting Small-scale Investigations in Educational Management,* London: Harper & Row, 79-92.

Ostrander, S. & Schoreder, L., *Super Learning 2000,* New York: Delacorte Press.

Shaw, G. & Ky, K. (1993). 'Music and spatial task performance' *Neurobioligy of Learning, Volume 6, 455-498, University of California, Irvin*

Shaw, G.(2000). *Keeping Mozart in Mind,* Academic Press, USA.

Staum, L.M., (1987). 'Music as an Intonational Cue for Bilingual Language Acquisition' *Applications of Research in Music Behaviour, Volume 6,* pages 45-60. Alabama Press : USA.

Tomatis, A. (1996). *The ear and language* Norval, ON Can

Chapter 2

Adaman, J.E. & Blaney, P.H. (1995). *The effects of musical mood induction on creativity, Journal of creative behaviour 95-108.* USA.

Harrer, G. & Harrer, H. 'Music Emotion & Autonomic Function' in *'Music and the Brain',* edited by Macdonald Critchley and R.A Henson, London: Heinemann Medical Books.

Jackson, M. (2005). *'Music to deter yobs'* BBC Music Magazine.

[3]Jensen, E. (2001). *Arts with the Brain in Mind,* USA: ASCD

[4]Jensen K.L. The effects of selected classical music on self-disclosure. *J Music Ther* 2001; 38 (1):2-27.

Johnson, G. , Petsche,C. , Richter, B. Filz von Stein,. (1996). 'The Dependence of Coherence Estimates of Spontaneous EEG on Gender and Music Training'. *Music Perception Journal No.23.: USA.*

Johnson, J.K.,. Cotman, C.W., Tasaki, C.S. & Shaw, G.L. (1998). 'Enhancement in spatial-temporal reasoning after Mozart listening condition in Alzheimer's disease'. *A Case Study. Neurol Research 20, 666-672.*

Lenhoff, H.M., Wang, P.P., Greenberg, F., & Bellugi, U. (1997). 'Williams Syndrome and the brain.' *Scientific American, December*, 68-73.

Mathews, S. J. (1806). *Effects of Music in Curing and Palliating Diseases*, Philadelphia: Wagner.

Meyer, L.B (1956). '*Emotion and Meaning in Music*, University of Chicago Press.

Shaw, G. (2000). *Keeping Mozart in Mind*, Academic Press, USA.

Stenhouse, L. (1979). 'What is action research?' (mimeo) *Classroom Action Research Network: Norwich, Volume 6, 211-215*.

Storr, A. (1997). *The Art of Psychotherapy*, London: Harper Collins

Swanson, J.M. (1992). *School based assessments and Interventions for ADD students*, KB Publications, Irvine, California.

[2]Yeoman, T. (2005). '*Music to deter yobs*' BBC Music Magazine.

Chapter 3

Black, S. (1997).'The Musical Mind', *The American School Board Journal*, January 1997, p 20-22

Brownley, K. A., McMurray, R.G., & Hanckney, A.C. (1995). 'Effects of music on physiological and affective responses to graded treadmill exercise in trained and untrained runners.' *International Journal of Psychophysiology.Volume 12, pages 16-18*.

References

Davidson, C.W., & Powell, L.A. (1986). 'Effects of easy-listening background music on the on-task-performance of fifth-grade children.' *Journal of Educational Research, 80(1), 29-33.*

[7]Goldstein, A. (1980). 'Thrills in Response to Music and Other Stimuli' *Physiological Physiology* 8/1 p136-29

Kemmis, S. & McTaggart, R. (1992). The Action Research Planner, (Third Edition) Geelong, Victoira, Australia: Deakin University Press.

[6]Meyer, L.B (1956). Emotion and Meaning in Music, Univeristy of Chicago Press.

Mockel, M., Rocker, L., Stork,T., Vollert, J., Danne.O., Eichstadt, H., Muller, R. & Hochrein, H. (1994). 'Immediate physiological responses of healthy volunteers to different types of music: Cardiovascular, hormonal and mental changes *European Journal of Applied Physiology, Volume 14, pages 25-36.*

Ponn R.B.; Silverman H.J.; Federico J.A.. Source: *The Annals of Thoracic Surgery*, Volume 64, Number 5, November 1997, pp. 1437-1440(4)

Scheel, K.R., & Westefeld, J. S. (1999). Heavy Metal Music and adolscent suicidality: An empirical investigation, USA Adolescence.

[5]Wilson, T.D. (2002). Information management. In J. Feather and P. Sturges, (Eds.), *International encyclopedia of information and library science*, (2nd ed.) (pp. 263-278) London: Routledge, 2002

Chapter 4

[8]Diehl & Stroebe, (1994). 'Brainstorming Groups in Context: Effectiveness in a Product Design Firm, *Administrative Science Quarterly, Dec 1996, Robert Sutton & Andrew Hargadon.*

Elbert, T., Pantev, C., Wienbruch, B., Rockstroh, B. & Taub, E. (1995). 'Increased cortical representation of the fingers of the left hand in String Players', *Science 270: USA.*

Farnsworth, P. (1969). *The Social Psychology of Music,* Iowa State University Press

Gardstrom, S.C. (1999). 'Music exposure and criminal behaviour: Perceptions of juvenile offender.' *Journal of Music Therapy, Volume 23, 116-125, USA.*

Henry, S.A., & Swartz, R.G. (1995). 'Enhancing Healthcare Education with accelerated learning techniques' *Journal of Nursing Staff Development 11/1: 21-24, USA.*

Hurwitz,I., Wolff, P.H., Bortnick, B.D., & Kokas, K. (1975). 'Nonmusical effects of the Kodaly music curriculum in primary grade children.' *Journal of Learning Disabilities, Volume 8, 45-51, USA.*

[9]J Gerlach, P Koppelhus, E Helweg, A Monrad - Acta Psychiatrica Scandinavica, 1962 - Blackwell Synergy 'Clozapine and Haloperidol in a Single-Blind Cross-Over Trial: Therapeutic and Biochemical Aspect (Angst et al. ... Psychiatric Hating Scale (BPRS) (Overall & Gorham (1962)).

Tharyll, W. (1994). *Using Rap Lyrics to Encourage At-Risk Elementary Grade Urban Learners to Read for Pleasure,* Practicum: Nova Univeristy: USA.

Took, K.J. & Weiss, D. (1994). *Heavy metal, rap and adolescent behaviour,* USA: Adolescence.

Wakshlag, J.J., Reitz, R.J., & Zillmann, D. (1982). 'Selective Exposure to and Acquisition of Information From Educational Television Programs as a Function of Appeal and Tempo of Background Music' *Journal of Educational Psychology, 74(5.* . 666-677.

Chapter 5

Boethius, A.M.S (1989) Fundamentals of Music, edited by Claude V. Plaisca, translated by Calvin M. Bower, New Haven & London: Yale University Press. p.8

Hughes, J.R., Fino, J.J., Melyn, M.A. (1999). 'Is there a chronic change of the 'Mozart Effect' on epileptiform activity?' *A Case study. Clinical Electroencephalography* 30, 44-45.

Campbell.J (1949) *The Hero with a Thousand Faces,* Fontana Press; New Ed edition

Levi-Strauss, C. (1970). *The Raw and the Cooked,.* London: Cape. P.18

Morrison, K.R.B. (1993). *Planning and Accomplishing School-Centred Evaluation,* Norfolk: Peter Francis Publications.

Sawyer. K (2007). *Group Genius: The Creative Power of Collaboration,* Basic Books

Took, K.J. & Weiss, D. (1994). *Heavy metal, rap and adolescent behaviour,* USA: Adolscence.

Wilson, T.D (2002). *Strangers to Ourselves: Discovering the Adaptive Unconscious*, The Belnap Press